Praise for

"What C-level executives read to decisions. Timeless classics for ina. Manager of Corporate Marketing Communication, General Electric

"Want to know what the real leaders are thinking about now? It's in here." - Carl Ledbetter, SVP and CTO, Novell Inc.

"Priceless wisdom from experts at applying technology in support of business objectives." - Frank Campagnoni, CTO, GE Global Exchange Services

"Unique insights into the way the experts think and the lessons they've learned from experience." - MT Rainey, Co-CEO, Young & Rubicam/Rainey Kelly Campbell Roalfe

"A must-read for anyone in the industry." - Dr. Chuck Lucier, Chief Growth Officer, Booz-Allen & Hamilton

"Unlike any other business books, *Inside the Minds* captures the essence, the deep-down thinking processes, of people who make things happen." - Martin Cooper, CEO, Arraycomm

"A must-read for those who manage at the intersection of business and technology." - Frank Roney, General Manager, IBM

"A great way to see across the changing marketing landscape at a time of significant innovation." - David Kenny, Chairman and CEO, Digitas

"An incredible resource of information to help you develop outside the box..." - Rich Jernstedt, CEO, Golin/Harris International

"A snapshot of everything you need to know..." - Larry Weber, Founder, Weber Shandwick

"Great information for both novices and experts." - Patrick Ennis, Partner, ARCH Venture Partners

"The only useful way to get so many good minds speaking on a complex topic." - Scott Bradner, Senior Technical Consultant, Harvard University

"Must-have information for business executives." - Alex Wilmerding, Principal, Boston Capital Ventures

www.Aspatore.com

Aspatore Books is the largest and most exclusive publisher of C-level executives (CEO, CFO, CTO, CMO, partner) from the world's most respected companies and law firms. Aspatore annually publishes a select group of C-level executives from the Global 1,000, top 250 law firms (partners and chairs), and other leading companies of all sizes. C-Level Business Intelligence™, as conceptualized and developed by Aspatore Books, provides professionals of all levels with proven business intelligence from industry insiders—direct and unfiltered insight from those who know it best—as opposed to third-party accounts offered by unknown authors and analysts. Aspatore Books is committed to publishing an innovative line of business and legal books, those which lay forth principles and offer insights that, when employed, can have a direct financial impact on the reader's business objectives, whatever they may be. In essence, Aspatore publishes critical tools—need-to-read as opposed to nice-to-read books—for all business professionals.

Inside the Minds

The critically acclaimed *Inside the Minds* series provides readers of all levels with proven business intelligence from C-level executives (CEO, CFO, CTO, CMO, partner) from the world's most respected companies. Each chapter is comparable to a white paper or essay and is a future-oriented look at where an industry/profession/topic is heading and the most important issues for future success. Each author has been carefully chosen through an exhaustive selection process by the *Inside the Minds* editorial board to write a chapter for this book. *Inside the Minds* was conceived in order to give readers actual insights into the leading minds of business executives worldwide. Because so few books or other publications are actually written by executives in industry, *Inside the Minds* presents an unprecedented look at various industries and professions never before available.

INSIDE THE MINDS

The Health Care Management Team

The Roles, Responsibilities, and Leadership Strategies of CEOs, CTOs, Marketing Executives, and HR Leaders

Published by Aspatore Inc.

For corrections, company/title updates, comments, or any other inquiries, please e-mail store@aspatore.com.

First Printing, 2006
10 9 8 7 6 5 4 3 2 1

ISBN 1-59622-483-5
Library of Congress Control Number: 2006903183

The Health Care Management Team

The Roles, Responsibilities, and Leadership Strategies of CEOs, CTOs, Marketing Executives, and HR Leaders

CONTENTS

Back to Basics: "Vision, Leadership, and Focus"

Dan W. Gladney

Chairman of the Board and Chief Executive Officer

Compex Technologies Inc.

Setting a Strategic Plan

The goal of a chief executive officer (CEO) should be to stimulate growth, foster teamwork, and create shareholder value. A CEO will want to have a few different methodologies in place in order to be successful. First, the CEO must have a vision for the company and possess the ability and resources to analyze his or her market, understand the trends, develop an idea, and orchestrate a strategy that will drive growth and profitability. The CEO and possibly key members of his or her team will meet with the board of directors on a regular basis and report on the company's performance in relation to their targets. At least once a year, the management team should meet in an effort to design or fine-tune their strategic plan. The process may last as long as three months, and each of the senior managers play a key role and take ownership in the plan and its direction. The plan should then be delivered to the board of directors for review and approval. Typically, the budget should be built after the strategic plan has been approved. A good management team will constantly revisit the plan and analyze their progress and determine if fine-tuning or a new strategic direction is warranted.

Leadership Plan

The development of a leadership plan starts with understanding where the company is, what it is capable of, and what stage the business is presently in. A company selling a mature product line in a mature, slow-moving market will have a different plan and focus than a company that is in early stages of research and development on their first product. For example, a company whose products revolve around a profitable but slow-growing physical therapy market may be very focused on distribution. The company recognizes their core strength, distribution, and may decide to launch their products in new, fast-growing markets such as orthopedic and pain physician clinics and offices. They recognize it's a different type of sale and may need a different type of leader to direct the efforts. On the other hand, the research and development company engineering their first product recognizes, based on their stage of development, the need to have a leader and leadership plan that understand how to strengthen relationships with thought leaders in the field listening and understanding to customer needs that will help define product development.

Implementing a Successful Plan

A successful leadership plan or vision is rarely developed by one individual. In a company with numerous employees, the CEO will want to be collaborative with the management team to both foster teamwork and to create new and effective ideas on how to make the company more successful. The CEO must work with the management team to come up with a realistic plan so the entire team feels like they are an important part of the process. They are the ones who will take the responsibility to implement the plan. The team has to decide together on the best choices for the company, the best route for the company to take, and then develop a leadership plan based on those choices.

Changing the Vision

A leadership vision can change depending on inside and outside factors in the environment. There are always outside factors that can change a strategy or vision. For example, a company may shift its strategy based on competition, pricing pressure, and evolving technology. A company that is the sole supplier of widgets may realize in three years that it has limitless competition and that the price of widgets has dropped substantially. That company may then branch out and start selling these same widgets into different markets or decide to develop new products that are related to their widget market. Internal factors that could change a leadership plan may be that the plan was established to improve the overall value of the company and stimulate growth, only to realize that the plan is not working. The customer may not accept the new product or service, or the company may not be able to stimulate growth as expected. This type of adversity must be dealt with in an effective manner, and it starts with recognizing that there is a problem and for every problem there is a solution. Therefore, to be flexible and creative plays a key role in the success formula.

Adversity is going to happen in companies. The CEOs and management teams who handle adversity effectively are the ones who are successful. The team should try to predict potential problems before they happen and establish initiatives that address these possible issues either in advance or immediately after they happen. Some people refer to this as "disaster planning." Keeping a cool head starts by keeping surprises to a minimum.

While it is obviously difficult to foresee what the future holds, not thinking ahead can lead to the loss of valuable time and money when a problem does occur. Start by asking yourself, "What are our strengths and what are our weaknesses?" From here, focus on the weaknesses and determine what could go wrong. Try this exercise with the management team and look at both internal and external factors that could impact your plan. You know the old saying, "If it could go wrong, it probably will."

Working Together

Cooperation among the senior managers is essential to the success of a company. In a public company, the CEO will work very closely with the chief financial officer (CFO) in order to make sure the company is fulfilling all of the compliance laws as mandated by Sarbanes-Oxley. The CEO will also work very closely with the CFO and all his or her managers in order to stay informed and aware. He or she will also work with the marketing and sales executives, as they have a dramatic impact on the top line. While the senior managers need to realize that the CEO has the final vote in the decision-making process, they must feel like they have the space and authority necessary to do their jobs. The CEO should work with all of the members of the senior management team on a regular basis in a collaborative manner. He or she should be respectful of their manager's knowledge, stay informed on the issues or concerns they have to deal with, and try to facilitate an open relationship. Everyone must recognize that nobody is perfect and everyone's creative thought processes are necessary to develop and manage a successful endeavor.

Team Skills

Every member of the senior management team should be a leader. They should also be an expert in their department so the CEO can rely on them to give the best advice and information concerning their area of responsibility. The senior management team must also be willing to work in a team environment where they may be asked for their comments or thoughts in other areas outside of their department. Creative thinking is not necessarily limited to the experts.

Working with Human Resources

The human resources department should work closely with the CEO to identify outside individuals who will make a great addition to the company. It is also the job of the human resources department to ensure that employees within the company can look to them for problem resolution pertaining to troubles with other employees or policy problems within the company. The CEO should be kept informed of any major problems or issues that arise with employees within the company.

Working with Marketing

The marketing department plays a key role in creating the marketing strategy for a business. The marketing strategy is particularly important because the company commits large sums of money to marketing. The CEO needs to be sure the marketing executive has an excellent handle on the market and the ability to deliver on the strategy. The marketing executive must also be incredibly knowledgeable on the capabilities of the product or service the company is positioning through their strategy.

Working with Finance

The finance executive clearly has to have not only a strong accounting background but also good leadership and communication skills. This individual works with every department within the company along with managing outside banks, and may be in charge of managing the investor base. The finance executive must work very closely with the CEO to ensure that the company is making sound financial decisions. The CFO must have a solid handle on the strategic direction of the company. A good finance executive will keep the senior management team well informed so that the team is able to make solid decisions the company will profit from.

Working with the Board of Directors

A CEO has to have a good working relationship with the board of directors. The CEO will want to inform the board of his or her vision for the company and involve the board in signing off on the strategy for the company. In most cases, a proactive board will help the CEO fine-tune the vision and strategy. I have always found my boards to be extremely helpful and focused on strategic issues. The CEO might even involve board members in the early stages of strategy development if they have a particular strength in certain areas. The CEO and the senior management team should make sure the members of the board feel like they were part of the planning process. A good board of directors is particularly adept in handling strategic issues and assisting the CEO in an effort to ensure the best possible return for shareholders.

Profit Strategies

There are two strategies I recently incorporated to strengthen profits. The first is easy: Cut expenses. You can accomplish this through attrition, layoffs, or cutting projects. The second requires a little more risk: Launch new products and/or expand distribution channels. Developing and offering new products might mean spending more to make more. It's risky, but in the long run you may end up with a faster-growing and more profitable company. Understand what your customers need and what they are willing to pay. Surround yourself with great people who can get you there.

CEO Challenges

The most challenging aspect of being a CEO in the health care industry is that a CEO must make sure a product is safe and effective. The product must also meet a clinical need and do it for less than the competition. Ultimately, the purpose of the product is to get a patient back to health faster and more effectively than the competition.

Long-Term Success

In order to have long-term success, a CEO has to recognize the company's core strength. The CEO must also be able to spot market trends and determine how the market trend will affect the company. Once the impact has been determined, he or she then can either utilize that trend to add value to the company, or if that is not possible, then create different technology to meet the needs of the market. However, in order for a CEO to truly be successful, he or she has to surround himself or herself with great people.

Advice for the Team

Team members need to communicate well with each other effectively in order for a company to be successful. It is also important that team members focus on the task at hand. Very bright people tend to use one great idea to start a project but lose interest after a certain amount of time and often switch to the next great idea. It is incredibly important that the CEO keep them focused on the project from the beginning to the end. Team members also must be willing to take personal responsibility for their actions. Team members should always feel a sense of urgency about their work. A company is in trouble if employees feel comfortable sitting back and watching the business flow. They should be aggressive in making sure the business continues to grow by individually taking responsibility to ensure that the company is the best it can be.

Difficult Situations

The biggest misconception of being a CEO is that people only see the title and the paycheck and do not realize the amount of work that went into attaining them. A CEO must be extremely focused, work incredibly hard, have a strong vision for a company, and work many long hours to put that vision into place. Every day, a CEO faces difficult situations. One of the most difficult is dealing with adversity. For example, a product may not be working correctly so a product recall may be necessary, or employees are not motivated to fix the latest problem in a problematic product. Another difficult situation is working with a productive employee who may lack people skills. The team has to believe they can accomplish great things by working together, and it is the role of the CEO to make that possible.

Retaining an Edge

It is important for a CEO to stay connected to his or her industry. A CEO does not tend to have a lot of extra time and may often rely on those he or she trusts, such as the board of directors, key managers, or business periodicals to keep him or her informed. It is also important to develop a network with other CEOs. While it might be difficult to talk openly with a CEO in the same industry, CEOs should at least try to speak with peers at CEO conferences to stay connected concerning important issues and debates.

Changing Role of the CEO

In the past few years, the role of the CEO has become much more collaborative. Many CEOs have started to recognize that they need to gather a strong team that can work together. Not only are good people important, but good systems are equally important. In the past, CEOs weren't as focused on the system as they were on making sure they got the best product and the best people. However, it is now necessary to ensure that good procedures and effective systems are in place. A CEO in the health care industry has to look at his or her company and products and be certain they are safe and effective as well as profitable. Improving shareholder value starts with a safe and effective product that delivers a clinical advantage at a value that surpasses the competition.

Three Golden Rules of Health Care

There are three golden rules of being a CEO in the health care industry. The first is to stay connected and informed. The second is for the CEO to surround himself or herself with great people that develop, manufacture, and sell safe and effective products. The third is focus, focus, focus.

CEO Advice

When a CEO sets about creating their own leadership or vision for a company, there are three important things for them to keep in mind. First, they should try to understand the trends of the industry. Second, they should try to have a handle on the customer base in order to determine what that customer needs. And third, once the CEO understands the trends and the customer needs, he or she needs to surround himself or herself with great people who are going to deliver on the plan.

Dan W. Gladney, president, chief executive officer, and chairman, joined Compex Technologies on September 3, 2002. He has twenty-four years of medical device experience. Most recently, he held the position of president and chief executive officer at Acist Medical Systems Inc. from 1996 to 2001, a manufacturer of high-tech cardiovascular devices. He successfully built Acist into a leading provider of automated contrast media injection technology for angiography and sold the company to Bracco SPA, an Italian pharmaceutical company in July of 2001. Prior to that, he held executive management positions at Cardiotronics, Baxter/Endomedix, Karl Storz Endoscopy, and the Kendall Company.

Mr. Gladney currently holds board positions with the following companies: Compex Technologies, Heart Leaflet Technologies, Incisive Surgical, and Neurovasix, all located in the Twin Cities area. Mr. Gladney holds a bachelor's of business administration degree from Eastern Michigan University. He has also completed M.B.A. coursework at Pepperdine University.

Defining the Role of a Chief Information Officer in Health Care

Shola Oyewole

Chief Information Officer

United Therapeutics Corporation

Introduction

The role of a chief information officer (CIO) is to provide a company with the best information technology (IT) tools available to assist the company in meeting its profit/loss goals. An indispensable CIO is the glue holding together the company. A CIO must not only understand technology, but he or she must thoroughly understand the business and how technology can be used to make the company more competitive. CIOs are the ultimate blending of business sense and technology.

Goals as CIO

As CIO of United Therapeutics Corporation, I strive to provide our company with the best IT tools available in order to accelerate our product pipeline to market. Telecommunications and computer technology are just a few of these tools. It is my job to always search for the latest and greatest available technology that will help us bring our products to market efficiently.

My overall vision and IT goals are to provide the best technology (computing and telecommunications) for the company to assist with what we do best: developing medicines for life. My goals are quite adaptive, as technology changes so rapidly. It is truly a daily changing process—one day a certain piece of technology might be cost-prohibitive to implement, and the following month it is suddenly affordable because of a breakthrough or shift in a manufacturing process. Of course, I cannot keep an eye on every piece of technology every day, but I do monitor certain ones on a daily basis. It is necessary to do this, since technology changes so quickly.

Many things I do have a direct financial effect on my company's bottom line. Meeting with technology consultants, attending trade shows to learn about new technology, and attending meetings are just a few. However, the most important decisions I make involve the actual purchase and implementation of technology.

The Art of Being a CIO

The role, and art, of being a CIO is to glue everything in a company together. This can only be achieved when the CIO understands the business of the company as well as the business leaders themselves. It's impossible for the CIO to provide a good solution if he or she does not fully understand the business.

A successful CIO must have certain personal qualities as well. He or she must be affable, very approachable, open-minded, and should possess qualities a good salesperson would have, since the role of the CIO is to speak in business terms and explain the business advantages of technology. At the same time, a CIO cannot use technology language—the days of technocratic CIOs are over. Nowadays, a CIO will sit on a board with the chief financial officer (CFO) and chief executive officer (CEO), who are both a step ahead in terms of business. CIOs may be playing catch-up in business, but we are doing our best to promote our causes and look for technologies that will help our business become more profitable. An effective CIO must be a business leader.

Personal Strategies for CIO Success

My company is divided into several divisions, and each has a head of office. At the first week of every month, a teleconference or televideo conference occurs where all major division heads meet to determine the challenges in the previous month and the challenges coming the next month and the rest of the year. These meetings allow me to prepare for any kind of effect these challenges will have on IT (or vice-versa). For example, in the research and development business of drug manufacturing, the Food and Drug Administration has stringent requirements that must be met by certain deadlines. These days, those requirements are affecting IT even more than ever. I must keep abreast of these requirements, and it helps to keep an open channel of communication with all parties involved so I can best explain the impact of these changes on our technological infrastructure.

My strategic meetings with my heads of office allow me to know in advance what their needs and goals are so we can in turn plan for the technologies they need to achieve those future goals. It is imperative for me to be proactive in assisting with these challenges, particularly since we are in the health care industry. Since the health care industry is heavily regulated, we must be as current as possible, and we must understand what the government requires of us. Although the government gives us time to prepare, CIOs in health care must be proactive because Food and Drug Administration and regulatory changes affect us very quickly and there can be expensive side effects if a company is not compliant.

Overcoming Challenges

The biggest challenge I face is translating technology into business terms. As CIO, I understand what needs to be done and how to get there, but I must sell this to the other business leaders in the company—the CEO, the CFO, and the other heads of offices—and in their terms. Sometimes, it is very difficult to explain the relevance of certain technologies. To overcome this, I am back in graduate school pursuing a master's degree in business administration. I sit at the table with these business leaders, and I want to speak the same language they do and have all of us understand each other. Fortunately, I do not face budgetary constraints; my company is very technology-friendly, and that is reflected in the technology budget. As long as the milestones/goals of the company are uppermost in mind, I am at liberty to implement whatever technology makes us remain competitive, accelerate our pipeline, and continue to provide "medicines for life."

Working with a Team

I work most closely with the CFO, his vice president of finance, and the CEO. As a public company, I know and understand that our financial goals are to maximize shareholders' value and remain profitable so we can develop more life-saving medicines. We are in the business of making medicine and increasing our pipeline in an economically affordable fashion. It is important for us that our medicines are successful and our company stays profitable. I strive to ensure that any technology solutions I propose comply with these goals.

The number-one goal for my IT team is to retain and maintain very high customer service standards. Checks and balances on this goal are very simple: If the customer is not happy, we'll hear about it.

The employees in the company have a very high regard for the IT department, and we work hard to earn this. We are very responsive to requests, and we log all item requests in our ticketing software. The logging includes the day and time of the request, and the system then tracks the progress of the request from start to resolution. Therefore, at any point in time I can generate a report and see outstanding tickets to determine what needs to be completed, what has been completed, and how it was completed. I also have regular conversations with the other heads of offices (COOs) to discuss how my department is doing.

CIO Strategies for Success

There are several things I have done to help my company grow and increase profits. With the benefit of technology, I have essentially "flattened" our company. What I mean is that the geographical separation of all ten or so major office locations does not impede communications, which is conducted electronically in real time. Since, in addition to the ten offices around the world, we have growing teams of virtual offices conducting business on the road twenty-four/seven, it is often difficult to foster communication due to so many different time zones and traveling schedules. To counteract this, I ensure that every staff member has instant communication capability through telephone PDAs, handheld computers, and any other Internet-enabled device. This contribution is significant to our bottom line, because it helps to bring our products to fruition very quickly in the sense that employees can work anytime and anywhere in the world at any hour of the day. They can communicate in real time and share documents and information quickly. Employees have access to the company intranet/extranet, which provides them access to real-time data on the company.

We perform research on new technologies as they become available (or as they are offered as beta products by the manufacturer), choosing what we determine to be relevant to our industry. We have test computers and several test labs where we set up test products—separated from the production system. This allows us to familiarize ourselves with these products to determine whether we indeed have a business need for such a product. If so, we will purchase it and plan a rollout with training sessions. The timeframe of the purchase depends upon the level of the product's relevancy and the availability of time to perform a proper rollout and conduct training sessions. We always talk to the vendors and make sure the technology has proper support. It is common that we review many technologies but do not implement them because of a lack of proper support.

To keep my edge and stay current on industry changes, I subscribe to a few text and online magazines. I conduct a lot of online research, and I review magazines catering to CIOs, CEOs, and bio-pharma research and development so I can gain an overall perspective of industry happenings. I also attend a few CIO and pharmaceutical seminars each year.

Misconceptions of CIOs

The biggest misconception about my position—and this is not unique to the health care industry—is that it is regarded as a very technical position. For example, if I attend a conference or an annual meeting, people tend to want to discuss technical problems with their home (or office) PC, and they look to me as a technical expert to help them out. I do not really mind, however, after providing them with good, technical advice, I change the conversation to pharmaceutical business. What are they implementing these days to comply with Food and Drug Administration rulings? What was their experience this year as they made their systems compliant with the Health Insurance Portability and Accountability Act? What pharmaceutical seminars or trade shows have they attended this year? What is their product pipeline like? How are their clinical trials coming along? What obstacles are they experiencing? What technologies are they implementing to capture data more efficiently? How did they handle their last Sarbanes-Oxley voluntary audit? The aim is to meld technological discussions with industry. I tend to learn more this way.

In addition, the CIO's division is considered a cost center similar to electricity or water. Rather, IT should be considered a strategic cost just like research and development or sales and marketing. In my company, technology is considered strategic for our growth. This is the case with most biotech drug development firms.

The CIO's Changing Role

The position of CIO has changed from being a highly technical position to more of a strategic business position. A few years ago, a CIO only talked about servers, antivirus software, and fighting technological vulnerabilities. Today, CIOs talk about IT in terms of leveraging their company's competitiveness and how it can help improve communications. In our company, we talk about how it can help us bring drugs to market more efficiently.

The Future of Technology

In the biotech/pharmaceutical industry, technological improvements have the potential to aid us significantly. For example, consider the genome. Although I am not certain of its current effect, its potential is enormous. Telemedicine, which is using technology to conduct medical procedures (invasive and non-invasive), is what truly excites me. I envision technology giving us the ability to have a doctor in the western world conduct surgery on a patient in a developing country using the Internet via satellite technology. The doctor would be in a lab controlling the remotely placed robot conducting surgery on a patient in the remote place. Or, consider a scenario where a mountain climber is injured while climbing in a very remote mountain and a robot could be dropped from a helicopter and then remotely operated to conduct surgery on the patient. Another exciting advancement of technology is to have a patient swallow a series of tiny camera-like devices—small enough to fit in the blood vessels—traversing the blood stream and capturing all kinds of information and reporting back in real time. This can help determine accurate locations of tumors and prevent future needless surgeries.

The Three Golden Rules of Being a CIO

The first golden rule of being a CIO is to learn to speak the business language as quickly as possible. The second rule is to never stop learning; learning is a continuous process, and it is impossible to know everything all the time, but a CIO must be current with technology and business methods. The third golden rule is to be a visionary. Since the CIO is the glue that holds all business divisions together, a CIO cannot be swayed by certain disturbing trends. A CIO must understand that these trends will pass, and he or she must keep a long-term view of the situation. Everything is temporary and eventually works itself out.

Conclusion

The position of CIO is crucial to a successful business. The CIO is responsible for ensuring that the company has the proper technology to achieve its business goals. A CIO is not simply a technical person; he or she is a strategic member of the management team and must thoroughly understand both the industry business and technology. By melding together business and technology, he or she locates solutions that help the company remain successful.

Shola O. Oyewole obtained his bachelor's of science degree in electronics engineering from the University of Ife, Nigeria, and went ahead to pursue a career in information technology in the United States while obtaining a master's degree in management information systems. For the past seventeen years, he has been actively involved in the information technology industry, working with a variety of firms (from steady nonprofits and government contractors to the more volatile dot.com startups). He has also consulted for the better part of the last fourteen years. He has a wide field of knowledge in the information technology industry.

Recently promoted and in his fourth year of employment, Mr. Oyewole is currently the chief information officer of United Therapeutics Corporation, a pharmaceutical and biotechnology drug development firm located in Silver Spring, Maryland. He is involved in decision-making involving companywide resources with complex, dynamic, and often ambiguous parameters.

Acknowledgment: *To Uloaku Echebiri, my fiancée, for helping edit this chapter.*

The Twenty-First-Century Chief Information Officer

Karen R. Kemerling
Vice President and Chief Information Officer
HealtheTech Inc.

The Goal of the CIO

First and foremost, the successful chief information officer (CIO) of a health care company will have a comprehensive understanding of the company's goals and an ability to adapt the technology needs of the company to these goals. For example, if technology is predominately viewed by upper management as a cost center, then the CIO must determine how to effectively function within those parameters; conversely, if technology is viewed as a strategic weapon for the business, there will be a greater willingness by the company to invest additional resources in its technical organization. In either scenario, it is the responsibility of the CIO to utilize the resources provided by the company to ensure that the available technology facilitates the most efficient operation possible.

In addition to recognizing the company's goals for information technology (IT), the individual serving as CIO must establish his or her own short- and long-term technology goals. In setting goals for the short term, there should be a primary focus on doing everything possible to facilitate the employee's ability to work at peak efficiency. This means keeping the day-to-day operations running like a well-oiled machine. For example, enterprise applications are up and functioning properly, the network and phone systems are accessible and providing acceptable throughput, and the company's information is protected from viruses and security risks.

The longer-term goals for the CIO should include a focus on implementing the necessary technologies to assist the company in maximizing revenue and sales objectives. This also means the CIO may be less of a "technologist" and more of a strategic leader who can understand the overarching company strategy and translate that into the best way to delivery the IT applications and supporting infrastructure.

The Challenges of Technology in Health Care

One of the challenges unique to the technical organization in a health care company is the necessity of maintaining compliance with governmental guidelines regulating the industry. Dependent upon the intended use and specifications of a device, there may be applicable regulations through the Food and Drug Administration as well as the International Organization for

Standards, which is an important component of most medical devices. In many instances, there must also be compliance with the Health Insurance Portability and Accountability Act, in addition to ensuring that all information held by the technology organization is secure from a record retention and privacy standpoint.

An additional challenge unique to health care is the need to work with current procedural technology (CPT) codes, which are a numeric system of codes designated according to the types of services a patient receives. Physicians and health care providers are typically only reimbursed by insurance companies, Medicare, or Medicaid if approved CPT codes have been indicated on all applicable forms. For this reason, most new products created in the health care industry should have an assigned CPT code or applicable associated CPT code before it will be used or recommended by health care providers. Any health care company wishing to market a new product typically lobbies for an approved CPT code; otherwise, the service is an out-of-pocket expense for the patient and typically used less frequently.

In addition to the above specific health care challenges, there are also some general challenges that apply to the CIO that are important to take into consideration. There continues to be a lack of understanding of technology by most business professionals. For this reason, the CIO must have the ability to address technology concerns from a business standpoint, which can often prove challenging. In order to achieve this, the CIO must convey the needs of IT in language that is easily understood by senior-level executives or other members of the company who may have little background in such matters. Alternately, the CIO must also have the ability to translate the business needs of the company into concise, realistic technology goals. Most importantly, the individual leading technology in a health care environment must have excellent communication skills and the ability to interact with employees and management with varying levels of expertise in the technological arena.

Maintaining the Company's Technology Vision

Because the market targets for health care companies can change frequently, the technological vision must be monitored and adapted on an ongoing basis. While the vision may be established on an annual or biannual basis, there should be monthly or quarterly evaluation meetings to examine the company's progress in relation to its established objectives. In those instances when it appears a significant change is occurring in the market, there may be a need to adapt the company's strategic plan to compensate for these changes. While it is rarely necessary to alter the vision drastically over the course of the year, there is always that possibility. For this reason, there must be routine focus on key market factors that may impact that vision. If you are monitoring these market factors on a weekly and monthly basis, technology course corrections can happen all the time, just in smaller chunks, which is more manageable and successful in the long run.

To that end, in order to determine the success or failure of IT projects, it is advisable for the CIO and his or her staff members to meet at the beginning of each quarter to determine how the goals of the IT organization will best contribute to the larger vision of the company. This is important for the entire IT organization, because it provides an opportunity for the CIO and his or her staff to focus on how each IT department will contribute to the company's overall goals. This is a cascading process where the CIO's goals will be split into smaller goals by department. In order to determine the success or achievement of these goals at all levels within the IT organization, it is imperative to agree on what a successful outcome of each project looks like. You must have an initial measurement or assessment of the situation and then the expected successful outcomes. The weekly checks along the duration of the project help ensure that the project is on track to achieve the agreed-upon goals.

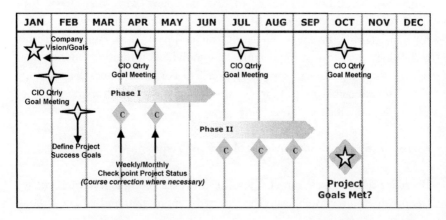

Throughout the course of any project, there must be an established process involving initial planning, development, implementation, testing/feedback, and then re-planning to apply the necessary updates. While the process itself is cyclical in nature, the CIO must establish a baseline measurement upon initiation of the project in order to determine whether the goals of the project are being met and contributing to the company's overall objectives. For example, the CIO has a quarterly goal to roll out a customer relationship management (CRM) system for a company's local and distributed sales force. In phase one, the project goals are defined: to have a functioning CRM system to track customer orders from the home office and from the road. The weekly checkpoint meetings incorporate updates and changes to the project as time progresses. In fact, one of the checkpoint meetings resulted in a change in direction, as the market showed that the remote sales force was not a good vehicle to generate sales, and as a result the remote portion of the CRM systems was not implemented. The end result of the project better met the needs of the company as the market and key goals changed.

CIO Staff and Relationships

It is imperative that all members of the technology team have excellent time management and organizational abilities, as there are frequently multiple ongoing projects that employees must manage simultaneously. Such organizational skills also come into play in determining how best to apply the appropriate technical expertise and abilities to a particular project.

In working with the IT team, the CIO must have an understanding of what motivates each individual. This may range from monetary compensation to recognition within the company or increased responsibility within the organization. By maintaining effective communication with employees and initiating discussions revolving around each individual's goals, the CIO will increase the likelihood of establishing a relationship based upon mutual respect in which the employee's goals are aligned with that of the company.

In addition to working with members of the technical team, the CIO typically works closely with a number of senior-level executives, including the chief financial officer (CFO) and the vice president of sales and marketing. The primary concern of the CFO is naturally the financial workings of each department; for this reason, it is common for this individual to view technology as a cost center requiring considerable resources from the company. Therefore, in order to work most effectively with the CFO, the CIO must take into consideration the return on investment for any project undertaken and must have the ability to convey the importance of each project in these terms.

In contrast, the vice president of sales and marketing is typically concerned with how best to understand the company's customers, as this increases the efficacy of each marketing effort. In order to facilitate this, the CIO may employ tools to determine which sales areas require additional personnel based on key demographic information, the efficacy of a particular marketing campaign, or which trade shows generate the most business. In working with this individual, the CIO's goal is to provide information that assists in making the best decisions possible with respect to which technical areas should be allotted funds to enhance the sales and marketing efforts of the company.

The Financial Impact of the CIO

One of the most valuable services the CIO provides for a health care company is to apply technology to improve and automate internal and external processes and applications, which results in increased accuracy and less need for manual processes.

For example, customer service may be handled through automated and self-service systems, thus improving the customer's ability to solve their own problem quickly and decrease the need for additional customer service employees. From the perspective of the CFO, such measures greatly increase the contributions of the technical organization to the company's bottom line for the short and long term.

The Process of Software Research and Development

One of the most important factors in effectively undertaking a software research and development project is to first understand the customers' needs and wants. To this end, surveys may be distributed, industry trends monitored, and key individuals within the market interviewed through the use of focus groups or other marketing strategies. The software research and development process then involves translating these findings into a determination of what is needed to meet the customers' needs (requirements) through the use of graphical/pictorial layouts, prototypes, and other technical specification. The next step of the process is to release beta software, collect feedback, update/refine the software per the feedback, and then release the software to the market. Once the software is released, the product is in maintenance mode, where fixes and updates are incorporated as needed.

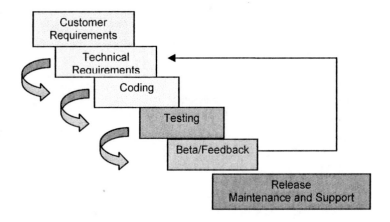

The Changing Face of Technology in Health Care

In recent years, individuals within the health care industry have begun to recognize the crucial role technology plays in a company's ability to efficiently meet the needs of the customer or patient. For example, as a result of Hurricane Katrina, there were a number of paper patient records that were lost when hospitals and nursing homes were destroyed. In the future, it will become standard procedure for health care providers to use technology to electronically store data in a standard format that can be accessed at locations across the country and the world.

Going forward, it is likely that there will continue to be an increasing amount of attention devoted to data security, such as how patient records are encrypted and who has access capabilities. As the number of doctors using handheld wireless appliances increases, it will be very important for technical teams to provide appropriate security to ensure patient confidentiality and data integrity.

Summary: Strategies of the Successful CIO

In order to be successful as a CIO in health care, as in any industry, you must first understand the goals of your company. Is IT needed to keep the appropriate technology working and maintained, or to provide new technologies to increase sales and service, or perhaps some of both? Understanding what the business needs from IT is the most important component in understanding how to be a successful CIO. Once you understand this, you must understand the capabilities of your IT organization and where you will need additional help, if any, to accomplish the company technology needs/goals.

Behind the scenes, there are several activities that enable a successful CIO:

- First, simplify and standardize IT processes plus equipment wherever possible. This enables fewer IT employees to more easily support the environment.

- Second, hardware and software contractual agreements should be scrutinized to ensure that they provide the most value for the company and are appropriately sized for its technology needs.

- Third, the CIO should also take the time to remain apprised of any changes in the industry in order to ensure that the company remains competitive. This may be achieved by attending seminars, taking part in various professional organizations, reading trade magazines, and speaking with both customers and fellow professionals in the industry. By maintaining contact with the customer, the technology professional has a better ability to understand and anticipate their needs in the marketplace. The successful CIO must recognize that technical and business factors change on a frequent basis, and therefore must have the flexibility to adapt to such changes.

Ultimately, the most valuable asset a CIO can have is the ability to effectively communicate with others, including members of the IT team, senior-level executives, investors, and customers. In those instances when a project is not going according to plan, communication often proves a valuable tool in maintaining morale, reestablishing a sense of control, and channeling energy in a positive direction.

Karen R. Kemerling Ph.D. has served as HealtheTech's chief information officer and vice president since March of 2003. She manages information technology, customer service, software development, and quality assurance. Prior to joining HealtheTech, Dr. Kemerling served a four-year term as the worldwide contact and business support manager for Agilent Technologies. Prior to her position at Agilent Technologies, Dr. Kemerling was with Hewlett Packard for eleven years performing a wide range of senior information technology management positions, including software development, infrastructure architecture, call center management, and disaster recovery planning.

Doctor Kemerling holds a doctorate degree in management with a focus on organizational development from Colorado Technical University, a master of science degree in management of information systems from Roosevelt University, and a bachelor of science degree in computer science with an electrical engineering minor from National American University.

High-Tech Medical Marketing: It's Not as Easy as Everyone Thinks

Clayton T. Larsen

Vice President, Marketing and Network Development

FUJIFILM Medical Systems

Introduction

Marketers in the health care industry face several challenges. Besides the general misconception that marketing is easy, marketers of high-technology health care products have a customer base that is highly knowledgeable, and a return on investment on marketing initiatives is difficult to quantify. However, certain strategies can help marketers in this field be successful. These include emphasizing marketing's role as a hub for all departments and striving to be the creators of the criteria by which all products in your category will be judged.

My Position

Marketing affects virtually every functional group in an organization from sales to service to product development; therefore, the goals of the marketing department must be a broad subset of the corporate goals. Our goals are the company's goals distilled. Though the immediately recognizable role of marketing is to "position" products and services, I believe our profession's role is to ultimately be responsible for positioning the company in the eyes of both the customer and the entire industry.

At our company, we manage three types of products: consumables, capital equipment, and software and software-related services. The consumables division consists mainly of the medical film used for all medical images such as X-rays and CT scans. With the market and technology forces of the last decade, this line has become relatively commoditized. The capital equipment product line comprises medical devices with a relatively high investment cost for a hospital or physician practice. The third product line consists of software and services related to acquiring, displaying, networking, and archiving high-resolution digital medical images. We do not separate these three lines into three divisions, because the same customer in the hospital is responsible for the purchase of all three categories. So we have aligned our company to manage these business lines simultaneously so as to maintain a consistent and unified image to our customers. The rate of change in our planning for these product categories is determined by the product type. A more stable, consumable, almost commoditized business will experience slow growth over a number of years, and marketing strategies will vary little if at all over a multi-year cycle.

In the capital equipment business, new products are introduced every year or two so that plans may have a one-year cycle. The software services business moves at a much higher velocity with nearly continuous innovation: Software products are released quite frequently. We need to be sure to reevaluate our marketing plans for this line quarterly to ensure that we are moving in the right direction and that our strategy stays consistent with new products, competition, and industry changes.

Defining the Playing Field

Some marketers use the classic features-advantages-benefits approach when positioning products. My philosophy for introducing new products, especially a new category of products such as our Web-based PACS introduced in 1998, is that we should take the time up front to organize and then communicate crisply what is the set of criteria for the whole market. These criteria must also be agreeable to the average customer as the most important things to consider when making a new purchase. We then demonstrate how our products fit those criteria better than anyone else's products. Instead of simply entering the playing field and competing, we try to first define the playing field. If a company can be the first to define the field, and the definition meets with the customers' agreement, the company's products will be seen as better suited to their needs. The company cannot fix the rules of the playing field in its favor; the customer would recognize that immediately, because again the general health care customer is very knowledgeable and discerning. The company must proceed carefully and examine the customers' needs. So when we introduce a new product, we think beyond its features, advantages, and benefits. We determine the global criteria we want customers to use to evaluate this class of products. If we ensure that they agree with our chosen criteria, we can demonstrate how our product meets those criteria better than the competitor's does.

Our customers are extremely intelligent people with an eye for detail. They perform important jobs and are trained to evaluate everything critically. Therefore, our approach is not as emotional as some marketing and advertising campaigns. We do take and have been successful with a humorous approach using eye-catching visuals; we try to get customers' attention as they read their technical journals. These highly educated, technically inclined customers are still human beings and can be reached on a psychological level with an eye-catching piece, but they will not be impressed by fluffy advertising and copy full of puffery—the end result must prove itself.

Challenges

No one would ever tell the chief financial officer how to balance a spreadsheet or tell the vice president of engineering how to write code or design a circuit board. Yet everybody thinks they have a good marketing idea and are not bashful about sharing it. So, it is a challenge to prevent the marketing department from being perceived as simply an idea chamber whose members never communicate with other people in the company. Marketing cannot be an island within the organization. At the same time, marketing is subjective by nature. The medical markets we participate in are not like consumer markets; they do not have the same statistically significant quantitative metrics. With the products we promote, it is difficult to link direct financial benefits (sales) to our marketing programs. This disconnect can affect whether marketing is perceived as valuable within the company and the budgeting for the department. So the chief marketing officer is challenged to ensure that others in the company know that marketing is listening and catering to both the customers and the internal constituents of the company.

There are ways to do this and ways I would not suggest. For advertising, for instance, I do not believe it is a democratic process to choose an ad concept or broader campaign. There are just too many subjective opinions outside the marketing department that would dilute the creative process. Collateral handout material, however, is extremely important to make sure there is an iterative collaborative input and feedback to ensure that it is a useful tool for field sales and field service staff who are in direct contact with the customers using these pieces.

Though marketing may appear to be easy, there is really an art to being a chief marketing officer. That art involves having the right touch in the right context. Sometimes one must be bold; other situations call for reticence and patience. The ability to assess a situation and act accordingly is where the right touch can gain advantage in the market. A good example can be found in overzealous product managers trying to perform a competitive analysis. I have found that a typical error in this effort tries to elaborate on many so-called differentiated features that give a laundry list of why a customer should buy our product versus the competition's product. Oftentimes, less is more and it is important to make sure our sales force can communicate the few "take-home points" extremely well, not an educational treatise on the whole field of technology.

The Marketing Team

Marketing must serve as consultants, reaching out to and representing the interests of other departments throughout the organization. We work directly with the sales force when we are introducing a product. The sales department is one of our major internal customers. Also, because we work in a highly technical field, we must communicate frequently, and at a rather technical level, with our engineers. Accordingly, some people in our department have extensive technical and clinical backgrounds. Our department also works with the employees who install and service our products. We must ensure that we engage that aspect of the business to confirm that our products, especially new ones, are installed properly and that customers are satisfied. Internal order management must also run smoothly: Prices should be quoted accurately and orders received and placed without problems. When new products are introduced, the right terms and conditions must be negotiated with the vendors of the product's subcomponents. Typically, we sell systems that include Fuji software and hardware, but also that of other vendors. We work with our colleagues in all of these areas of the company so we can understand ahead of time the issues of primary importance to them so the release of new products can proceed as smoothly and quickly as possible when it reaches their functional responsibility. We need to understand the other tasks they may have on their plates as well as what their management has put as their incentives. As the famous office sign says: "Lack of planning on your part does not constitute an emergency on my part." Marketing needs to make sure the timing of new products is not a surprise to anyone in the organization.

Being able to accomplish all that is outlined above—working with other departments and representing other interests—is no small task and requires constant attention to detail. That's why I expect members of my team to have certain skills and qualities. One is content knowledge. In clinical and technical matters, team members must be equally knowledgeable as both our customers and our sales force are, if not much more so. They need to train the field sales, and any trainer needs to know the content better than the trainee. When issues get referred to "corporate," customers expect a higher level of knowledge than found from the local representative. I also value the ability for a person in my group to want to learn. I value people on my team who want to learn from me and from others, as well as from the competition and from their own mistakes. This, in my estimation, is one of the most important components of success.

Because we go to the same events and trade shows each year, and our team is experienced, we focus not on what we need to do each year but on what we should do differently. Changes in resources or market conditions or the introduction of new products can alter our goals. Members who have been in similar roles for a number of years can introduce some element of complacency or lack of an "edge." Recently, we implemented a method to increase our productivity by changing the function of the marketing communications team. When the product team owned the majority of responsibility for deliverables, long delays could be experienced due to competing urgencies. We set the expectation that the communications team would be more involved in the execution of campaigns instead of the product team alone. Now, both the product team and the communications team know the goals in advance. If one group is falling behind schedule, I will likely hear about it. Under the previous system, I relied on the product group alone; if they fell behind, I'd be less likely to know about it because they might not wish to point out the delay to me. Now, two groups are equally accountable for bringing a product to the sales force, an industry trade show, or the customers, and I receive early warning of any problems.

Strategies for Growth

When a company is selling software in a high-velocity product area that is experiencing customer- and industry-induced changes, it needs to strike a balance in terms of "selling just what we have" versus revealing the future and products to come. Customers need to have a look at the horizon and the plans the company has for the future in order to be confident of the roadmap ahead. This is particularly the case when you sell a software product that needs to change to help customers adapt to the changing needs of their practice and workflow. But the company should not sell the future as if it is available today. If it does, the customer will not be satisfied with the product they purchase, and receivables will be a problem. If future features are communicated poorly during the sales process, the customer may withhold final payments for large system projects until they get that feature. At the same time, customers need to know the company's roadmap to compare the company against the competition. The trick is to ensure that customers understand the potential of the product's architecture and the company's plans without promising a specific timeframe for deliverable features that might affect the company financially.

Another important strategy to sustain growth is to focus on ongoing support for upgrades of the installed base. Analyzing our particular industry over the past ten years, we have seen a leadership ebb and flow run in cycles. A company would develop a good product and become successful in the market, then experience a downturn. This downturn inevitably resulted from the company's failure to maintain its installed base and keep its existing customers satisfied. In order to avoid this historical mistake, we have tried to interrupt this cycle by disciplining ourselves to include "evergreen" clauses with our required software maintenance agreements. An evergreen clause represents a future revenue stream, but more importantly, customers will be more satisfied three or four years after the purchase because their product will continue to be state of the art by regular periodic upgrades. Many customers like the thought of making a long-term investment but are shortsighted and ultimately buy on price when choosing among competing products. We have maintained the software maintenance contract as a requisite component of our business: It is good for us, and ultimately it is good for the customer.

Misconceptions and Problems

One of the biggest misconceptions that exist concerning my position is the idea that marketing is easy, and that anyone can do it. Marketing always has to prove its worth, and one way that can be practically measured is by how often we are sought after for support. We sell capital equipment that has a high average sales price, so our sales force is seasoned. If they cannot see how marketing provides benefit to them when selling the next deal, they do not place much value on including marketing. If someone from marketing is sought after by the sales team, that means he or she is doing a good job and is seen as adding value. The misconception stems from the myth that marketers just throw together some ads and brochures while sitting around drinking lots of coffee; in reality, marketing is a vibrant hub of activity across technical and financial domains where many functional groups must interact.

Having a dissatisfied sales force is not a good situation for a chief marketing officer, but an even more difficult situation I have to handle in my position is when a customer is not happy. Often, this is due to poor execution on our part, and the problem escalates until it reaches my desk or the customer calls me. It is important to handle these situations properly because in the health care business, our customers are dealing with patients in critical situations. But because these problems are often caused by a complex set of factors, I must be careful not to unfairly criticize members of our organization, as the customer may be and often is partly to blame. I must balance the customer's sense of urgency for answers with a methodical, fact-gathering approach.

Resources

One of our most useful resources is the agencies we use and the people who work there. These people are extremely knowledgeable, and they understand the context in which we are working. Occasionally, my staff will bring me an advertisement or brochure in which, after reading it carefully, the product is not being positioned properly. The logic of the release is flawed because someone in the process did not understand the product, the market, or the goals of the company. The people who add value to an organization are those who can understand marketing situations and apply that understanding in a number of small ways that are collectively significant. A wrong decision about positioning can have larger consequences. We have observed this with our advertising agencies. For example, if the agency mishears a minor point during a debriefing, they may come back to us with concepts for an ad campaign where that one misunderstood point might now be a central part of the campaign. Also, as mentioned previously, having the right touch is important. Because marketing is a subjective enterprise, we tend to create better campaigns and position products more successfully if we simply follow the basics of making good decisions based on good targeted information.

Changes in the Industry

In the coming years, there is no question that changes in the health care industry will affect how we operate. These changes include increased attention to medical errors and adverse events among patients and the move toward "pay for performance." The criteria for the outcomes for our products will be set by the industry. We will have to be able to demonstrate to customers how we can help them achieve those clinical outcomes that will be mandated by both regulatory and reimbursement bodies.

The most memorable piece of advice I have ever received from another chief marketing officer was a baseball analogy. He said that, just as good pitching always beats good hitting, good marketing will always beat good engineering. That's because marketing can lie about the product faster than engineering can ever build it. I found it funny, and even close to home for other companies I've competed against in my career. In health care, however, no product can stand on marketing alone, and an engineering-driven company with strong marketing is the best of all worlds. As long as the engineers don't make suggestions for ads...

Conclusion

Marketers in all fields must deal with the common misconception that marketing is dispensable. Those who market health care products face additional challenges, including a highly educated customer base that cannot always be targeted in traditional ways, and future regulatory developments that will make reaching desired health care outcomes more critical. To succeed in the face of these challenges, marketers must promote their departments as listening and catering to the multifaceted needs of the company. They must also focus on understanding the customer and maintaining customer support post-purchase.

Clayton T. Larsen was appointed vice president of marketing and network development at FUJIFILM Medical Systems USA Inc. in 1998. In this role, he oversees all marketing and communications activities for Fuji's successful line of conventional and digital diagnostic imaging products, including Fuji Computed Radiography and Fuji's SYNAPSE PACS.

Mr. Larsen joined Fuji in 1996 as managing director of marketing. In the following years, he was instrumental in the development, marketing, and commercial release of Fuji's PACS. He has also introduced a number of key innovations at Fuji that have been influential in changing the way a PACS is purchased and deployed. Under his guidance, Fuji has pioneered a completely Web-based PACS system, software-only PACS installations, and concurrency-of-use payment for software licenses.

Prior to his work for Fuji, Mr. Larsen was employed by Acuson Corporation for eight years, last serving as vice president of new market development. From 1981 to 1988, he specialized in sales and marketing of ultrasound and nuclear medicine for Picker International.

Mr. Larsen holds a bachelor's degree in molecular biophysics and biochemistry from Yale University. He was previously presented with the International in Awe Award for marketer of the Year by the Medical Marketing Association.

Think Like a CEO with the Customer as Your Boss

Claude Hooton

Executive Vice President, Sales and Marketing

Baxa Corporation

My overriding goal as chief marketing officer (CMO) at Baxa is to use state-of-the-art methods to create a world-class sales and marketing organization. As part of this initiative, it is important to me that my team is excited about coming to work each day and that they believe in the significance of what they are doing. Every year, there is one defining rule for our company: BTSP, or beat the sales plan. My good friend and mentor Walter Spath taught that to me early in my career, and it has proven to be effective many times over the years.

In many ways, I view the company in the same way I view my daughters. With respect to both the company and my children, I want to provide a solid foundation in education, training, and guidance that enables them to excel at whatever they do. I also try to help them set goals beyond levels they ever thought were possible. At Baxa, we have always had very ambitious goals and have exceeded them all.

Goals and Strategies for Marketing in the Health Care Industry

Although I have worked in the health care environment for over fifteen years, I have also had the opportunity to work in a number of other industries. What I have found is that the fundamentals of business are essentially the same regardless of what markets you are serving. Regardless of the field, it is always critical to work with your customer as a partner to first determine what the needs are. At that point, it is up to the sales and marketing team to develop and implement solutions that address and resolve those issues.

There are, of course, nuances specific to health care. As in any industry, the successful marketing person must possess a great deal of domain knowledge in order to be successful. This is not necessarily true for other functional areas. Having worked for a year in accounting, I can safely say that accounts payable is an accounts payable, regardless of the industry. Marketing requirements, on the other hand, vary significantly from industry to industry. As an example, certain products must comply with the Food and Drug Administration's specific guidelines. These regulations affect the product from inception through production, all the way to its use in a clinical environment. The discipline required to follow these rules is much stricter in health care than in other markets. Penalties for non-compliance are swift and onerous. Beyond its business ramifications, non-compliance can lead to the death of a patient. This is something with which health care marketers must deal. I have worked for two separate companies that have had patients die as a result of misuse of our product. Although it was not our fault, such events have a profound impact on a personal level; ultimately, I have found this spurs an even more intense dedication to one's work.

Updating the Marketing Vision

I believe the marketing vision should change about every three to five years. In contrast, the fundamental corporate mission is something that is the bedrock of the organization and should not undergo much change at all. With regards to the marketing plan, I believe it is very important to set five-year strategic goals that supply the path to reaching the vision. On an annual basis, the one-year goals help the company to take a significant step along the path towards success. Ultimately, the amount of change to the marketing plan directly correlates to the timeline of the plan. The longer-term goals usually do not undergo significant modifications, while the annual plans tend to be more fluid.

The Art of Being a CMO

The art of being a CMO comes from realizing that, essentially, it is not an art. I believe it is more of a science. Even marketing communications, which is perceived as the most creative component of marketing, requires a strict compliance to objectives and a formal process of organizing the message. Sales is the same way; we are organized by and adhere to a process called "value selling." Value selling provides a guideline on how to organize a sales cycle with a potential customer. This includes listening to what the customer's issues are, defining the problem and potential solutions, developing a plan of action with key milestones, and, perhaps most importantly, providing defined steps where the cycle can be terminated if it does not make sense to move forward.

Where the art comes in is in the ability to decipher through the noise and pinpoint where the important issues and opportunities are. I have heard customers and product managers describe great opportunities without even realizing it. The artist sees these things immediately.

Of course, to be successful as a CMO or chief sales officer, one must have a passion for what he or she is doing. We are often leading the company and our customers into new areas. There are always challenges and obstacles along the way, and as a result, there will always be times where it just does not seem to make sense to continue. However, if it is a good concept, you begin to see successful results, which is one of the most rewarding feelings in this job.

While passion is important, it must be coupled with good analytical thinking. I love the saying that "hard data drives out soft." In order to rally the company or our customers behind an idea, there must be compelling data to back up an idea or concept. More often than not, recommendations and ideas are based on gut assumptions. However, the value proposition must be quantified in some way. My undergraduate and graduate degrees are both in the area of finance. I have found this, coupled with my passion for the field, to be very helpful as a marketer and sales leader.

Strategies and Methodologies for Achieving Success as CMO

The most important marketing strategy is to actually have one. It is interesting to note how few marketing professionals have three- to five-year plans. Once you take the first, most critical step of realizing the importance of having a strategy, there are a number of basic strategic elements you can put in place. I have developed a few basic methodologies I have used at a number of companies across a range of industries.

One strategy involves thinking like a chief executive officer (CEO). I always tell our product managers that they are the presidents of their business lines. I look to them to figure out how to make their products successful. They need to track their key metrics monthly just as if they were managing a company. They need to rally the team regardless of whether the team consists of sales, product development, or key customers. The idea of thinking like a CEO germinates greater responsibility and bottom line dedication to each task and goal.

Another important strategy is to focus on making money. The dot.com craze emphasized the damage that can result from basing a business model on good ideas that are not profitable. The most successful products have an annuity stream associated with them. In other words, the money is made on the razorblades not the razors. The value proposition must be clear and quantifiable. "Nice-to-have" products and services are always beaten out by "must-haves." It is our job to clearly communicate why what we are offering is a "must-have."

Further, set goals that are aggressive, important, achievable, and quantifiable; then develop and monitor metrics to ensure that you are achieving these goals. Part of this strategy involves spending time in the field with customers and the sales team, as this interaction enables CMOs to understand what goals are achievable and how best to monitor the team's progress.

Ultimately, a very important part of any marketing strategy is to build the best team possible. My job is actually very easy because I have an excellent team. If there is a weak link, it is the role of the CMO to figure out how to help that person improve or, alternatively, guide the employee to find a place where he or she will be successful. This does not always mean terminating them from the company. One of our best moves was to take a sales representative with mediocre performance and promote him to head up our field operations and support. He is now in the right position and doing an excellent job.

When building the team, I believe a successful health care marketing organization needs a diverse set of skills. While I always look for the best person in terms of capabilities and fit with the organization, I have found that the ideal group has a mix of analytical M.B.A. types, people with field-based sales experience, and highly innovative members from our customer base—preferably with experience using our product(s). As with a sports team, the interchange among the members must be a productive one. Even though we always look for stellar individuals with great talent to offer, there is no room for a star who cannot work with and contribute to the team.

The three basic things any CMO can do to have financial impact on and add value to his or her organization is to work as a member of the leadership team to set the long-term strategies and goals; develop a plan with key members to implement those strategies throughout the organization at the operating level; and BTSP, beat the sales plan.

The Most Challenging Aspects of Being a CMO

There is never a dull day in marketing. Every day, there is a new demand from one stakeholder or another. I tell our product managers that they have the worst job and best job in the whole company. I have worked in almost all functional areas, and I have learned that managing your time in marketing is unlike doing so in any other department. I have never known a product manager who can come into work and actually execute what he or she had planned for the day. There is always an urgent customer issue, a sales representative who needs your help, a supply chain issue, or some other urgent matter that surfaces unexpectedly and takes up their time.

Another key challenge is maintaining positive and productive relationships with all of the respective functional areas of the company. Marketing and research and development have a natural friction in their relationship with each other. Research and development is trying to develop a reliable product in as short a time frame as possible. Marketing wants the best long-term solution. Meanwhile, sales wants to begin selling yesterday. I have found that consistent and continual communication must occur among these groups. I have made it a point to personally have an excellent relationship with our vice president of research and development. As a matter of fact, we have become great friends and spend time out of the office running marathons together. Relationships like these provide critical avenues for maintaining successful communication among departments, ultimately empowering different parts of the company to work together to achieve success.

Strategies to Grow Your Company

At several companies, I entered the corporation in the midst of struggling divisions or product lines and turned them around. Although I have an M.B.A. from Harvard, the fundamentals I call upon to deal with challenging marketing situations actually come from my "Introduction to Marketing" class at San Diego State University. I follow the basic rule of marketing and closely evaluate the four Ps: product, place, promotion, and price. If any one of those areas is weak, you cannot be successful.

One example of the benefits of focusing on the four Ps occurred with a company that had experienced unprecedented success as an innovative company. Pyxis Corporation had revolutionized the way medications were dispensed in the hospital. Our main product, Medstation, was similar to an ATM, only it dispensed medications on the nursing floors. The company was the fastest-growing public company in America for two years in a row.

Along the way, customers asked for a bigger cabinet in which to store larger items. This was the genesis of the Supply Station. When I came on board, the Supply Station's revenues had declined for three years in a row and the program was headed toward extinction. After meeting with the supply team and with customers, it was evident that the Supply Station was wrong in the Ps department.

First of all, the *product* functionality and the area in which it was being marketed was wrong. The supplies used on a nursing floor are low in cost and do not need to be controlled. Part of our value proposition was to reduce inventory consumption and levels. Consequently, there wasn't much value to be had there. The average dollar consumption in a week was about $600. It took time to gain access to these items, so the nurses had actually figured out ways to pilfer the inventory from the cabinets and hoard it in their own little stocking areas.

On the other hand, the operating room and the catheter lab had large inventory values. Furthermore, a stock out of inventory could cost tremendous time and money as well as potentially put a patient's life in danger. We decided to target this area.

The product offering had to change. As you can imagine, there was significant interface required to implement this type of change. While people did not mind going through a number of steps to get to a medication, they did not want to go through all of those steps in order to get to a supply. In some cases, the supplies were on huge metro carts in the operating room stores room. In order to address this market, we completely redefined the way in which items could be removed. We also changed the size and configuration of the products. We even made a mobile cart for the anesthesiologists to use. All in all, we developed eleven new products in less than two years.

We next had to change the way we *promoted* and implemented the systems. The representatives who were selling the med station knew a lot about the pharmacy and the medication supply chain but knew very little about the procedure areas of the hospital. In response, we hired a twenty-person dedicated materials services sales team and a thirty-person field service team. All of them went through a two-week "boot camp" training session on the specific needs of this specialized market.

We also changed the *price* to reflect the value proposition being provided. We developed a low-cost system to manage the low-value items while also providing a higher-priced automated cabinet to manage very high-value items such as implantables and catheters.

As always, it comes back to BTSP, beating the sales plan: We not only beat the plan, but we blew it out of the water. After years of declining revenues, we had close to 100 percent growth in the first year we implemented the specialized products and field team.

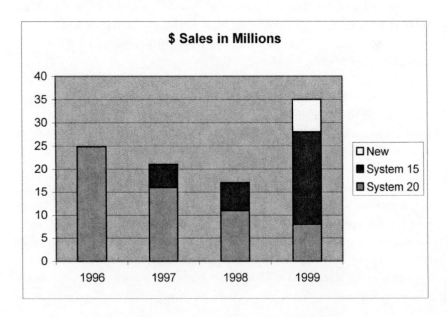

The Biggest Expenses of a CMO

As the head of sales, marketing, and service, my biggest costs result from the expenses associated with the sales organization. To balance this, our marketing expenses are relatively low. We primarily spend our marketing funds on headcount and promotion. With respect to promotion, we focus on marketing communications and public relations. We are a well-established, thirty-year-old company with an extremely strong brand among our target audience. Consequently, we are able to put most of our emphasis on promoting new products or services. We have an excellent in-house creative service team that produces great collateral and promotion pieces.

Any time we look at spending additional money, we always look at the value of what we are spending as well as the return. We will usually pilot a program before spending a large sum of money on it. One example is using a road show with an opinion leading speaker, which we recently tried doing for a new product. We had great success and, as a result, subsequently funded a whole series of them the following year.

Biggest Misconceptions about the Role of CMO

I have met very few non-marketing people who fully understand the depth of what any role in the field involves. Many people think marketing simply involves developing marketing communication pieces. Still others believe marketing is all about product development. Even more common is the misconception that sales and marketing are synonymous. These roles are clearly different.

I believe many of these misperceptions exist because so much marketing work is done in the background. People do not see all the pricing meetings or the large focus group studies taking place. Production planning begins with a sales forecast from sales and marketing. All of this takes place in meetings behind closed doors, and the finished collateral pieces or products are only a small portion of the work involved in the marketing process.

Resources and Advice: Getting an Edge in the Marketplace

In order to stay current and maintain an edge in the marketplace, I regularly read a number of trade and industry journals that keep me apprised of new trends in the industry. I learned early in my career that one should spend at least thirty minutes per day devoted to this type of education. I have had a great deal of formal education, so I spend most of my time now learning from the market. Above all, I make sure to speak frequently with customers, our sales representatives, our marketing team, and our field support team. I have found that these contacts are my most valuable resources.

Throughout my career, I have always been a member of a rapidly growing company. What I have come to realize is that there is always going to be stress associated with this type of expansion. What I try to do is identify that this will happen early and often. I stress to team members that we are all in this together, so they will never find themselves without a support team. However, the group needs to be ready to change on a moment's notice. This can often translate into moving from one priority to the next and to scrub many hours of work.

I also stress that we will make mistakes. If we are not pushing the envelope, we are not going for breakthrough performance. I try to set up a culture that allows people to venture into new areas without the fear of failure.

The other key piece of advice I share with my team is that it is impossible to over-communicate. I truly believe this, although I am not talking about simply sending more e-mails. I am referencing face-to-face (or at least phone-based) communication. Most of the problems with which we are faced could be solved by simply picking up the phone and calling the person with whom we have an issue. This goes for both internal and customer issues.

In turn, I have received some solid advice from other CMOs as I have gone through my professional adventure. Early in my career, I was asked to think like a customer. In other words, always ask myself: "What will a customer think when they see our advertisement? How will they react when they hear our value proposition? How will my product make their lives better?" I do not like to waste my time listening to irrelevant sales pitches. Our customers are just like us. All of our customers have personal issues in their lives. They have an internal political structure at their institution. Even though they may want our technology, they often cannot afford to risk their job with a new concept. We need to partner with them to help them further their business as well as personal goals.

The Coming Years: Changes in the Marketing Field

In the past, one could rely on fairly tried and true marketing tools. Collateral material presented the products, advertising helped get awareness up, and a little direct mail helped stir things up. In the 2000s, the noise level has dramatically increased. We all get barraged with e-mails from all directions. The amount of direct mail I get at home and at work is ridiculous. In order to be effective in the future, CMOs must fully utilize state-of-the-art technology to streamline the way they get their company's message out. The key is to provide a simple and powerful message in a highly sophisticated manner. For example, we do not typically use PowerPoint in our presentations. Rather, we use a very interactive electronic presentation tool similar to a Web site without all of the text. This allows us to tailor every presentation to exactly what the customer wants rather than showing thirty irrelevant slides. We simply click on the relevant topic and go directly to it.

The use of e-mail as a communication forum is paramount. However, it must be very profound and valuable to the reader. We use permission-based e-mail campaigns that are driven from characteristics supplied by our customer relationship management system. This allows us to surgically target exactly the right audience with each campaign.

Three Golden Rules of Being a CMO

There are three basic rules that are critical to success as a CMO. The first is to create solutions that will lead to big value for your customers by providing solutions that make the company significant money. The next is to spend at least 20 percent of your time in the field with customers. This keeps you aware of their needs and hones your communication skills to enable you to interact effectively. Finally, build the best team possible and devote the necessary time and money to keeping them.

As the executive vice president of sales and marketing for Baxa Corporation, a thirty-year-old global medical device company providing solutions for the preparation and administration of liquid therapies, Claude Hooton is responsible for worldwide sales, service, marketing, and business development. During his time at Baxa, Mr. Hooton has exceeded sales forecasts every year with average annual sales growth in excess of 25 percent. He has grown revenues from $39 million to $91 million and was responsible for growing market share in the automated TPN compounder market from 12 to 70 percent.

While with Baxa, Mr. Hooton was recognized by American Business Awards for having the best sales organization in the United States. Prior to Baxa, Mr. Hooton was the executive vice president of marketing and corporate development at SupplyPro Inc., where he was responsible for marketing, strategic planning, and business development. He has also held positions at Pyxis Corporation, Dura Pharmaceuticals, NCR, and IBM Corporation.

Mr. Hooton attended Harvard Graduate School, where he was awarded an M.B.A. in general management curriculum with an emphasis in corporate finance. He holds a B.S. in finance from San Diego State University, where he was a four-year member of varsity crew.

Happily married with four children, Mr. Hooton remains active in a number of outdoor activities and has completed six marathons over the last three years. He is the past president and officer of Harvard Business School Club of San Diego and a member of the chief executive officer group with the Executive Committee.

Building a Team to Effectively Market Scientific Products

Gregory J. Gosch

Vice President, Marketing and Sales

Luminex Corporation

Introduction

My goal as a chief marketing officer (CMO) is to define and execute marketing and sales strategies targeted at growth in revenue and profitability. Secondary goals are ensuring that the voice of the customer is resident in product development, creating broad awareness of company products among customers, and continuously building brand integrity.

Unique Strategies

We have a unique business model. Unlike our competitors, we license our technology to companies with core competencies in vertical markets. These partners build applications that leverage our technology and sell them to end users. Thus, our strategies largely revolve around enabling our various partners.

Leadership Plan

The vision rarely changes. The strategies and tactics to accomplish the vision, which might be called the leadership plan, change more frequently. The frequency is dependent on the level of success of a given strategy or tactic. I'm a huge fan of measuring return on marketing activities whenever possible. When starting a new concept, we often shotgun the activity, measure the results, and then redirect resources in a very focused way on the activities that performed well during the shotgun.

For example, we recently decided to have a larger presence at trade shows as part of a brand awareness strategy. In the first year, we invested in more than twenty different shows and measured the activity at each (booth activity, leads, etc.). We have now focused the effort to less than ten shows and applied a majority of our investment to six shows where we have a very large presence. Sometimes, hard measurement numbers are available (e.g., the number of Web hits or e-mail responses to a campaign). Other times, only soft measurements are available (e.g., opinions, limited surveys, etc.).

In general, a marketing plan should be reviewed at least quarterly, and tactics should be adjusted as necessary. The overall strategy should have a comprehensive review annually if measurements indicate that the strategies are working, but more frequently if measurements indicate that they are not.

Adding Value

As the CMO, the most significant measures I undertake that have a direct financial impact and add value to the company are: define customer-oriented product requirements, establish pricing, and build (or leverage) relationships and open dialogue with key opinion leaders.

Define Product Requirements

Collect and deliver the customers' requirements to the internal product development group and successfully negotiate the creation of a highly competitive product within reasonable timelines and at competitive costs. Most critical here is collecting requirements from those customers who influence the purchasing behavior of a majority of the market. Often, these are not the more obvious "thought" leaders who speak at conferences and publish in journals (who are often more interested in more feature-laden, complex, and therefore expensive products). Rather, they are those who are more pragmatic and seek for a limited array of useful product features at a competitive price. These are customers who are more interested in purchasing products that improve their work productivity rather than just having the latest technology. Their peers look to them when trying to identify the next generation of technology that will improve work efficiencies. These customers can be challenging to identify and often only found through careful observation of customer purchase patterns and surveys. Once found, they can be a very efficient source for competitive customer product requirements and can become crucial advocates of a new product.

Establish Pricing

Some companies in our industry rely on cost-based pricing. On average, companies target a 50 percent margin on equipment sold and a 75-plus percent margin on reagents. By so doing, they sometimes price products too high to be competitive, significantly limiting market penetration. Other times, they may price products below what a customer is willing to pay.

This limits company revenue and profits that could be used for investment in future products. It also does a disservice to the company's investors. The most successful businesses in our segment, large or small, price products based on what the market will bear (as best as they can) versus on an internal margin requirement. This may be a simple business concept, but in actual practice can be difficult to execute. Determining value-based pricing requires a higher level of analysis and testing— for example, evaluating the impact on downstream health care costs when pricing an upstream clinical diagnostic test. In this situation, many variables must be considered including: the treatment decisions a physician has following a diagnostic test, the health and financial impacts of these decisions, and the impact of making an incorrect decision based on poor information versus a correct decision based on superior information. The greater the health impact of the decision, the more critical, or higher value, the diagnostic result. The higher value the result, the higher the price the market will bear.

Build (or Leverage) Relationships and Open Dialogue with Key Opinion Leaders

This is important for setting up good customer requirements, but it is also crucial for market adoption. Getting products into the hands of key influencers is paramount to broad success. As mentioned above, identifying these key influencers is more challenging than some may think. They are not necessarily those who publish the most papers or speak at the most conferences. In fact, many of these customers do not adequately represent the market as a whole. Rather, it is those who are first to adopt a technology once it has demonstrated to provide improvements over existing technologies. These select customers better represent the broader market and will be much better at helping define marketable product features and creating awareness of new products in the marketplace. They can be hard to find, as they are not as visible as the early adopters. Once found, however, they are golden contacts. Strong relationships with them represent a key competitive advantage. Once they adopt and/or endorse a product, their influence on the larger market is priceless.

Being Successful

To be a successful CMO, you must truly understand the customers' needs and effectively communicate these throughout your organization. In turn, you must also understand your company's product strengths and your unique value proposition, and effectively communicate these to customers.

A CMO must also be analytical as well as bottom line-oriented. And this means knowing what the numbers mean and how to impact them. He or she must not take a limited "sales today" approach with the mistaken assumption that one important customer represents the needs of all customers. That kind of knee-jerk reactive product development approach to meet the demands of the most recent customer phone call is a recipe for disaster (and it happens). The data from many customers need to be evaluated in the aggregate, and the impact of various investments needs to be analyzed. The CMO must use the data to educate and persuade in-house developers toward building real-world competitive products.

A CMO must be an excellent communicator. Marketing works with all other corporate departments and must do so effectively for the company to succeed. The CMO must champion the product cause and create excitement. The CMO is also a company brand advocate who must create excitement among the customer base and do so with credibility.

Unique Aspects

In the health care industry, reimbursement and regulatory oversight are unique aspects of my work.

Reimbursement

Those who use our product are different from those who pay for our products. Our end users depend on the government and insurance companies to reimburse them for clinical tests. This removes all the parties from classic market dynamics. Without these dynamics, it is more difficult to predict and influence purchasing decisions. For example, most patients would rank "high-quality care" above "cost" when asked about their own treatment. However, those paying for that treatment (insurance companies and other third-party payers) have demonstrated a willingness to sacrifice at least some level of quality if it means saving a significant amount of cost. Thus, product providers in the health care arena struggle to meet the quality needs of the patients and physicians yet maintain the cost controls demanded by third-party payers.

Regulatory Oversight

Depending on the diagnostic test, the Food and Drug Administration has various levels of oversight and approval required. This oversight is to ensure an appropriate level of product quality among health care products. Obtaining approval requires testing on the part of the manufacturer. At its extreme, the testing can take many months or years post-product development and cost hundreds of thousands, sometimes millions, of dollars. In many cases, this testing and approval is required prior to marketing the product. Additionally, due to rapid scientific advances in clinical research and the subsequent regulatory modifications to testing guidelines, it can be a daunting task to keep up with and adequately comply with new guidelines. Regarding marketing, the Food and Drug Administration is particularly sensitive to "performance claims" made in reference to a product. Marketing must balance positioning statements and selling points in various sales tools to ensure regulatory compliance while also adequately highlighting the product's capabilities.

Teamwork

A CMO needs to be both a strategic team leader and a savvy team player. As my company's CMO, I am both a member of the executive management team and the leader of the marketing team. Key to any team's successes are strategic leadership, clearly defined objectives and goals, and, most important of all, qualified, strong team members. The skills I value most in team members are:

- Ability to energize others
- Ability to lead without appointed authority
- Integrity
- Intelligence
- Independence
- Excellent communication skills (both one-on-one and in larger audiences)

Regarding team goals, we have a rigorous objectives-based system that establishes five to six key, measurable objectives that must be accomplished within a given deadline of the year. Progress toward the objectives is discussed at least monthly with the employee and formally reviewed quarterly. The objectives are position-based, and a weighting is applied to each depending on its importance. Many project team members share the same objective in an effort to unite the team toward the same outcome.

The Future

Market research is key to making informed decisions. However, market research reports can be expensive, costing thousands of dollars. Often, only one or two sections of a report are relevant for specific analysis.

In the last couple of years, several competing online services have made market research reports available. A key to this new approach is that users can purchase parts of a given report rather than the whole document. This allows us, with the same amount of investment previously required for a single report, to canvass specific sections in four to five reports for similar or lower cost. Triangulating the market numbers this way provides more confidence in the final estimates. Two services that offer this are: Dialog Profound (dialog.com) and MarketResearch.com.

Webcasts are also a very useful tool. In health care, much of marketing involves packaging and crisply communicating the science. Most end users in our markets are intrigued by new scientific products, so creating curiosity is not our biggest challenge. However, often these customers have one or two questions or points of confusion keeping them from trying the new products. Webcasts are an excellent method for clearing confusion and answering questions; Webcasts allow companies to sponsor Internet broadcasts by experts. E-mail lists allow invitations to go out to targeted audiences at minimal cost. The Internet allows the speaker to present from the comfort of their own office and the attendee to listen at an equally convenient location. Webcasts can also be archived and posted on the company Web site for later view should any attendees have a schedule conflict.

Misconceptions

The biggest misconception in our industry is that marketing isn't needed until late-stage product development. Many companies have an "If we build it, they will come" philosophy. They are science- or engineering-driven and see marketing as a late-stage process not required as part of upfront development. This is particularly true at startups. Often in new scientific company ventures at the executive level, the corporate executive staff will include a chief executive officer, a chief financial officer, a chief scientific officer, a vice president of business development, and legal counsel. The marketing executive is often recruited just prior to commercialization. "We need to bring someone in to launch the product," say the board members and executives. The realization that the technical staff didn't understand customer requirements as well as they needed to is often painfully evident at product launch when many of these companies begin scrambling to modify the new product to better meet customer needs. Smarter companies bring in marketing early on in an effort to gain a better understanding of the customers and market prior to and during the early stages of product development.

Even in some established companies, research and development drives the product idea and development process. Without well-coordinated customer input, these companies often launch products that need multiple rounds of revisions post-launch before they gain any market acceptance and become successful. Again, having marketing involved from the initial stages of development could help avoid some of this rework.

The second-biggest misconception is that marketing activities take little time to execute and don't need to be initiated until the end of the product development cycle. To be done correctly, the marketing launch activities must begin early in the product development cycle. In fact, because many marketing and product launch activities involve engaging outside resources, these activities can take longer than those items the company has internal control over. For example, when beta testing a product, marketing must coordinate with the calendars of outside customers willing to beta evaluate a particular product. If testing at multiple sites, it's often not possible to coordinate all of these sites at the same time due to prior scheduling commitments the outside customer may have. An effective launch process should begin simultaneously with the product development process. Then the plan can accommodate the following: having outside papers written on the product; market awareness advertising prior to launch; trade show coordination and public relations to prepare the market for the product; introducing the product or concepts to key influencers; carefully evaluating the competition; and side-by-side competitive comparisons, to list a few.

Conclusion

As more products crowd the market, marketing is becoming more sophisticated. The biggest change to marketing scientific products in the coming years is the Internet. We anticipate this will continue to grow as the medium of choice for marketing. Companies are developing virtual trade shows on the Web (with booths, product displays, etc.) in an effort to make product analysis more convenient. Key scientific and clinical journals are seeing more of their customers using the Internet version of their publications (versus the traditional paper subscriptions). In some recent surveys we conducted that asked customers where they look first for product information, the Internet was a resounding number one (versus a journal article, sales representative contact, trade show, advertisement, or other). For scientific products, this represents a significant change in the information channel and thus a shift in how we need to market products. We expect this trend to continue and are investigating new ways to focus resources on the Web to promote and educate customers about our products.

Gregory Gosch is the vice president of marketing and sales at Luminex Corporation in Austin, Texas. Mr. Gosch started his career in hospital administration and then moved into the medical equipment industry. His marketing experience began at Bio-Rad Laboratories, where he was an account manager and then moved into product management. His career since has focused on molecular diagnostics and life sciences research. Prior to joining Luminex, he held global marketing and sales leadership positions at Chiron Diagnostics and Nanogen.

Mr. Gosch has an M.B.A. and a master's of health care administration from the University of Minnesota, and a B.A. in molecular, cellular, and developmental biology from the University of Colorado.

Medical Device Marketing

Dennis Rosenberg

Vice President, Marketing and International Sales
VNUS Medical Technologies Inc.

Increasing Visibility in the Marketplace

The role of the medical marketing professional is to propel the company's products to increased visibility in the marketplace. For some products, the marketplace may include both the professional marketplace of physicians as well as the consumer marketplace of potential patients. The goal is to turn that increased visibility into increased sales for the company. Ideally, to achieve this visibility, a mix of marketing, advertising, and promotion vehicles are combined into a unified program. Key elements of a medical marketing program may typically include trade shows, journal advertising, consumer television, print advertising, direct mail, workshops and events, customer training and clinical support for users to maximize utilization, and e-marketing and Web site strategies. To maximize the positive financial impact and return on investment, careful testing and monitoring of the different programs guide the mix of program dollars. Maintaining the big picture, 30,000-foot view is crucial in crafting the most effective message in the marketplace.

Marketing in the Health Care Industry

The sensitivity to maintaining best medical practices should always be in the forefront when planning marketing strategies and methods. In terms of marketing to physicians, it is important to keep in mind that your products and techniques are the tools of the trade for saving or restoring people's health. To reach physicians, the most effective marketing vehicles are medical conferences, direct mail, training programs, Web sites, hospital events, journal advertising, and clinical publications. Fielding a direct sales force, participating in trade shows, and developing other advertising and promotional opportunities are extremely expensive. The uniqueness of the health care industry is that the patient's health is always what is at stake. The right medical decisions for each patient are the highest threshold, with the goal of providing the best care possible.

Evolving Vision

To some degree, the marketing vision should be updated with feedback each day, but a focus on longer-term goals must be consistent. Basic direction should change infrequently, but keeping in touch with trends in evolving modalities of patient treatment, new technology, basic science, research advancements, and other areas of the marketplace are also important. A classic example from cardiovascular medicine is the dominant role coronary stents grew to play in the treatment of coronary artery disease during the 1990s. Many devices and entire modalities fell by the wayside as clinical results increasingly pointed to the dominance of stents. The fortunes of many companies and investors were made and lost during this period.

CMO Qualities for Success

In order to be a successful chief marketing officer (CMO), it is essential to maintain a sense of humor in the face of the seriousness of the task. Accurately evaluating quickly changing scenarios and situations must be performed daily, but always in the context of the larger view. Balancing sensitivity toward the patients themselves, who are dealing with their own health issues, attitudes and opinions of physicians, and the economic conditions of the health care industry is usually challenging but always crucial.

While the physicians themselves are the number-one marketing consideration, the CMO must also carefully consider the strengths and weaknesses of their own company, their product, and their internal team. The CMO must have the vision first to see clearly, and then the flexibility to integrate successfully, all of the realities of their situation.

Clinical expertise is invaluable, which is a consideration beyond any found in the marketing of most strictly consumer goods. A deeper knowledge base is required in the marketing of medical devices than is needed for selling cars or packaged goods. Staying up to date means attending medical conferences, reading the medical journals, industry newsletters, and consumer press, as well as constantly monitoring the trends reflected by opinion-leading medical specialists. Medical device marketing results are directly affected by the level of success in blending scientific and medical knowledge with awareness of the basic sales process and consideration of fundamental human nature, all fueled by an ongoing entrepreneurial spirit.

Teamwork

The marketing team works closely with sales, finance, engineering, research and development, product manufacturing, legal, and clinical and regulatory colleagues. Marketing invariably finds itself at the crossroads between many disciplines, typically working closely with every department within the company. Regulatory considerations are very important, as they are the fundamental driver of the medical indications and product claims that can be made for specific products. The clinical side is where the "rubber meets the road" and is where the answers to the most essential questions are revealed: How well are the products working? What are the most effective ways to use the products? Monitoring the clinical use of the products and realistically evaluating their strengths and shortcomings ultimately falls within the marketing function.

Hard work, diligence, enthusiasm, intelligence, sensitivity, knowledge, and a sense of humor are essential qualities of the marketing professional. The larger company goals filter down into the specific measurable goals within each department, and marketing's role is always primary in a successful company. Depending on the maturity of a particular company and its product development pipeline, a typical set of measurable goals might relate to the number of successful product introductions in a given period of time. Another example of a measurable goal might be the success in generating a specific number of physician inquiries about a particular product. The key is to distill the broad corporate goals into a set of specific marketing goals that can be benchmarked by specific metrics to track success.

Unique Responsibilities

Medical device marketers must follow the dictates of the marketplace, as in any other industry, but within a framework of mandatory regulations from the Food and Drug Administration, the Health Insurance Portability and Accountability Act, the Centers for Medicare and Medicaid Services (formerly the Health Care Financing Administration), the International Organization for Standardization, and the Sarbanes-Oxley Act of 2002 (for publicly held companies), as well as voluntary guidelines from groups such as AdvaMed, which serves in part as an industry watchdog group. It is extremely challenging to integrate the different goals, responsibilities, and regulations found within the health care industry. As an appropriately highly regulated industry, we must set specific and measurable goals that are an appropriate balance between the overall company strategy and objectives and the industry constraints. The company goals filter down on a department by department basis, and relevant milestones allow these goals to be measured appropriately.

Advice for Health Care Marketers

Listening to doctors is the number-one priority for medical device marketers. It is also essential to read the key medical journals and keep up to date with other professionals in the industry. People tend to become overwhelmed with the constant temporal and financial pressures, yet in order to be successful, it is important to regularly take a deep breath, relax, and maintain a healthy perspective of how each action fits into the context of the larger picture.

Changes in the Role of Marketing

Medical device marketing seems to become more regulated each year. For example, new restrictions on direct-to-consumer marketing are now being put in place that are more restrictive than those in most other industries. As a result of these restrictions, the freedom to operate has been lessened.

The rapid pace of development of new medical devices, procedures, and techniques will have a significant impact on the future of marketing. New products will expand the market with new approaches, while others will make conventional techniques easier, faster, or less expensive to perform.

In the future, it will continue to grow more challenging to attract and maintain the attention of doctors through traditional marketing techniques, and new forms of outreach will be constantly evolving. The growing trend toward e-marketing strategies is a good example. New communication channels and tactics will continue to be innovated.

While medical device marketing will continue to be primarily driven by clinical data, the impact of health care economics will increase not only on the marketing function, but on product development itself.

Golden Rules of Marketing and Sales

Here are some golden rules: Listen intently to doctors. Watch demographic and social trends. Hire people smarter than yourself. Successful hiring is both the hardest and the most important thing you can do to make an impact. After evolving past the limited impact of being a sole contributor, you realize the real power in leveraging the impact other people can have. The better the people you hire, the more powerful your lever becomes. Harnessing this effect has a huge impact on the scope and success of your marketing efforts. The intelligence, insight, and skills of your individual contributors are multiplied by the overall commitment of the team to a common goal. The result of this equation is what drives the success of medical device marketing.

Dennis Rosenberg joined VNUS in August of 2005 as vice president of marketing and international sales. From 1999 through 2005, Mr. Rosenberg operated his own marketing communications company, Metaphor Media. Concurrently, from 2002 through 2004, he served as a consultant to Acueity Inc., a micro-endoscopy company, operating as acting chief marketing officer. From 1997 through 1999, Mr. Rosenberg served as vice president of marketing and sales for MD DataDirect, an Internet information company. From 1995 through 1997, he served as vice president and general manager of Randomsoft, the software distribution division of Random House, a publishing company. From 1989 through 1995, Mr. Rosenberg was a co-founder and vice president of marketing and sales of Eclipse Surgical Technologies, a laser medical device company, and concurrently from 1990 through 1992 served as vice president of marketing and sales for Atlantis Catheter Company, a cardiovascular catheter company and spin-off of Eclipse Surgical. From 1987 through 1989, he was sales director of MCM Laboratories, a laser medical device company.

Mr. Rosenberg studied film and television production at New York University.

Dedication: *Dedicated to Kate, Alex, and Annie.*

Tailoring Marketing Strategies to a Specialized Health Care Market

Michael Stone

Executive Vice President

Schick Technologies Inc.

This chapter focuses on one marketing approach to a small specialty health care segment: the professional dental market. The dental industry is distinctive for two reasons: the characteristics of the primary consumer (i.e., dentists) and the unique sales channels that are available to manufacturers in this industry. Since these factors vary widely from country to country, the following describes our successful experience and strategy within the largest single dental market in the world: the United States.

The Audience

The first step is to understand the audience. The professional dental market is unique in U.S. health care. In the United States, there are about 140,000 dentists operating out of approximately 110,000 locations. Dentistry is a precisely defined universe, predominately owned and operated as small sole proprietorships. It is important to understand that upon graduation from dental school, most dentists have little or no training or experience in business management, yet they must operate a small business. They are fearful of making a poor business decision, and they often look to other dentists or their local dental product sales representative for advice regarding new technologies and product purchases.

Also, most dental offices are "fee for service" and do not face the same pressures that exist in other areas of health care due to capitated payment systems, such as health management organizations. Since most practitioners work alone, the efficient use of their time is a critical element to profitability. Unfortunately, for want of traditional business education, many dentists do not appreciate the role a return on investment analysis plays in the decision to purchase new technology. Because dentists tend to look at what a product costs and not what it returns, a traditional business-to-business approach is inadvisable in dentistry.

The Offering

As a second step, it is critical to identify and understand your product offering. This is not always as obvious as it first seems. For example, we manufacture high-quality digital radiography sensors. These sensors replace dental X-ray film in much the same way that a consumer digital camera replaces traditional film. The advantages are both obvious and numerous;

reduction of radiation dose, elimination of toxic chemicals, increased production and efficiency, resulting in a rapid return on investment. Clearly, digital radiography is an innovative product that delivers real benefit.

However, our experience has taught us that dentists do not buy digital sensors. They buy instant chair-side imaging. They buy the ability to communicate with and impress their patients with advanced technology. They buy a means to make their daily lives less stressful and more enjoyable. Identifying this as our product offering was key to developing our marketing strategy.

The Channels

The third step is to understand how your choice of channel affects your offering. In a small industry like dentistry, careful channel selection is a key part of a successful marketing strategy. There are three traditional channels used in dental equipment sales: direct, value-added resellers, and dealers. Most dental equipment manufacturers sell through a network of dealers.

When I first arrived, our company was selling on a direct basis and incurring huge sales and marketing expenses because of it. At first glance, a direct sales force may seem attractive due to the potential for increased margin. But the enormous amount of advertising needed to provide leads is very expensive, and providing comprehensive local support is not feasible under this model. Ultimately, we were spending way too much money and giving away the product too cheaply under the direct sales method.

Our high-tech product must interface with other products existing in the doctor's office. We need people on a local basis to integrate and install and deliver the product so everything works in harmony. The problem with working with many different dealers, or even a direct sales force, is that there is potential for inconsistency of after-sale service and skill from one region to the next. The value-added resellers channel suffers from the same problem. A solid infrastructure across the nation is necessary in order to achieve a seamless result.

Another disadvantage of using a multiple-dealer network is price competition. When a product is available to the dentist from more than one source, the possibility for "price shopping" exists. This ultimately devalues your product in the eyes of both the dealer (due to less-than-ideal margins) and to the end user (who now thinks of it as a commodity versus a premium product).

In order to remedy the problem, we increased the price by 250 percent and went from a direct sales force to a distributor arrangement by forging an exclusive distribution agreement with the largest dental distribution company in the country. Through this arrangement, the distribution company agreed that they would create the infrastructure needed for service and support after the sale as well as during the sale of the product.

Reasons for Choosing the Exclusive Distribution

Our decision was to sell exclusively though a single dealer capable of covering the entire United States. When this decision was made, it was widely considered to be unusual, even risky. But, because we understood our offering and our audience, we were confident it would work for us.

First, dentists are used to a level of handholding from their distributors on a daily basis. Therefore, the distributor is a critical element in dealing with these doctors. These dentists get very comfortable with services of the local distributor, and they become dependent upon that relationship. In more recent years, the larger dental dealers have become "business partners" in the sense that as a small businessman, a dentist can look to a dealer for sound advice on everything they need to know about setting up their business: where to locate, leasing, even office design and construction. The dental dealer sells them every piece of equipment, monitors every transaction, puts everything on one lease document, and finances the entire process. This leads to a very strong long-term business relationship between rep and dentist. In fact, we consider the rep to be "the gatekeeper," since they have such a vested interest in protecting the dentist's business.

Even though our sensors are technically superior, we realized that the best way to communicate our real offering (i.e., trouble-free, instant chair-side images) was through these gatekeeper relationships. By going exclusive, our dealer gained a premium, high-demand product with protected margins. In return, our dealer provides all after-sale support for our product, thus making them an integral part of the "trouble-free" offering. This level of commitment from our dealer, with their strong gatekeeper relationships and their ability to service our product locally, is a key component of our offering that gives us an advantage over our competitors who sell direct.

Marketing Strategies

The main goals of marketing are to create a strong brand and to build the channel and relationships that are necessary to deliver the final product to the end user. It is important to start off with innovative products that can deliver benefits. Then, the idea is to formulate a unique proposition with our channel partners and create a franchise around those products to bring to the customer. Our advertising/placement strategy is very specific. Our primary goal is to inform and motivate our dealer partners to present our product to their dentists. To this end, the objective of our placements is to maintain visibility to the distribution channel.

At the time I arrived, the category was stagnating after a period of rapid growth. Because we were in the unique position of being the category leader, we realized that the best way to increase sales was to grow the category. The logic was to convince more dentists to buy digital radiography, knowing we would get the lion's share of the new business. Had we tried to sell our brand versus the competition, we would have failed to see the growth we were looking for.

We maintain our brand and our positioning by attending and sponsoring many trade shows and educational seminars. These are excellent opportunities for us to interact with our customers and dealer partner in an environment that sets us apart from our competitors. These venues work well to reinforce our dealer relationship, as well as build the category— exactly the type of exposure we want.

Financial Strategies

Price positioning is the first step toward instigating financial impact. If you don't have the right price, you don't have the right margin. If you don't have the right margin, you won't make a profit. The second step toward financial success is surrounding yourself with the right talent, meaning internal employees, to execute your plans. No matter how good the plans, without execution, the profit levels will not be ideal. The third necessary step in creating financial success is to form good relationships with channel partners. It is critical to secure the services of another party that has an infrastructure strong enough to deliver the rest of the proposition to the customer.

Challenges

One of the early challenges we had was the speed at which our exclusive distribution partner was able to "ramp up" sales. The role of our sales managers has always been to coach and motivate our partner reps to sell our product. In these early days, however, they were also expected to close orders themselves. This was important for two reasons: It gave us the financial cushion we needed until our dealer was up to speed, and it gave individual dealer reps the opportunity to see firsthand how our products positively affected their dentists.

Building the right team can be a challenge. High-integrity, high-energy people are ideal members of a marketing team. Product managers should be able to bridge the void between engineering and marketing. These specialists must be technical enough to explain to the engineering team how they are going to create the product. In terms of sales management staff, leadership is the most important factor. Our salespeople manage a field sales force of approximately 1,400 people, each of which has different roles and responsibilities. These very diverse sets of people have to be managed effectively, so flexibility is critical.

One risk that is always a factor is technological innovation by the competition. We mitigate this risk by investing heavily in our own research and development and aggressively protecting our intellectual property. Senior members of the organization attend all major trade events, both domestic and international, to assess developing trends and to keep an eye out for the next opportunity.

Conclusion

In summary, it's important to decide if you will employ a "pull strategy" where a major advertising campaign is used to create sales leads or a "push strategy" where the idea is driven through the local distributor sales force and their strong relationships with the customers. It was the incredible strength of the distributor relationship that made this decision simple for us. With an average of over ten years calling on the individual customers, the distributor representatives had developed many sole-source accounts where they literally were supplying every need, almost like outsourcing materials management. Buying capital equipment from the distributor that supplies so much of the day-to-day materials creates leverage, as the salesperson will work hard to make sure the customer is happy.

Michael C. Stone is the executive vice president at Schick Technologies Inc. a publicly traded manufacturer of medical devices, primarily for dental X-rays, located in Long Island City, New York. Mr. Stone has over twenty-five years of experience in the medical device industry, with various management responsibilities in sales, marketing, and general management. Prior to joining Schick, he spent thirteen years at Welch Allyn Inc. in Skaneateles, New York.

Mr. Stone holds an M.B.A. degree from the University of Rochester. He is also a member of the executive advisory committee at the William E. Simon Graduate School of Business Administration at the University of Rochester.

The Changing Profile of a Health Care Marketing Professional

David A Russell

Vice President, Global Marketing, Patient Monitoring

Philips Medical Systems

The Role of Marketing in a Health Care Company

As vice president of marketing of a leading health care company, my goal is to not only maintain our position as a global competitor in the development of patient monitoring equipment, but also to continue to grow the company by developing new technologies for the future. In any health care company, the individual who leads marketing efforts cannot be satisfied with simply meeting company goals in the present; he or she must always look toward the future and determine how to exceed present goals while simultaneously taking measures to ensure that the company remains competitive going forward.

To achieve this, the vice president of marketing must have significant industry knowledge so he or she can accurately predict what needs will arise in the market to determine how the company may best meet these needs. The company with the ability to read current market trends, anticipate future and often unspoken customer needs, acquire the required technology to meet optimally those needs and work aggressively to ensure that they are the first to make this technology available to the customer stands the greatest likelihood of success in the short and long term.

Growth in the Area of Patient Monitoring in Health Care

There is an increasing desire within health care organizations to treat critically ill patients as quickly as possible in order to limit the time spent in intensive care units, as treatment in such units is exceedingly costly for providers and patients alike. The proliferation of monitoring requirements that have resulted from this need to move patients out to lower acuity hospital settings earlier than was previously the case has triggered growth in the area of low- and mid-acuity patient monitoring equipment in the health care market. Today, there is also significant demand for high-level monitoring equipment that increases physician efficiency, particularly as a result of the shortage of health care providers in the industry.

When working in patient monitoring, one is extremely close to the end user and the patient, as most equipment is used directly by the health care provider, whether a nurse, intensivist, anesthesiologist, or surgeon. The patient's well-being is dependent on the ability of the manufacturer to guarantee that the technology will work reliably at all times, thus increasing the responsibility of the vendor to design the most dependable, advanced equipment possible.

In order to enter successfully the area of patient monitoring, a company must be led by an experienced team of professionals with a comprehensive understanding of the global health care industry. This is particularly important when navigating the multitude of national and international medical regulatory requirements, such as those of the Food and Drug Administration in the United States and the JTA in Japan. While this area is currently one of growth, only those companies with the knowledge, experience, and technological ability to execute the design of such equipment with high efficiency and efficacy will gain the reputation necessary in the market to become a global leader or can retain their global leadership position.

The Value of a Diverse Portfolio

A health care company must have a winning solution portfolio in order to gain significant market share without sacrificing bottom line profitability. This may be achieved by ensuring that all practices are undertaken in the most cost-effective manner and by keeping in mind that the most desirable outcome for any company is manufacturing at high volume. Whenever possible, appropriate sourcing should be done on an international basis to ensure that the cost of manufacturing is minimized without compromising quality or performance.

The vice president of marketing is integral to this effort, as it is his or her responsibility to ensure that the company gains market share by expanding the product portfolio in a productive and profitable manner, specifically by introducing the company's products and expanding the product portfolio to new or untried adjacent segments of the market. When the company has established itself as a highly respected, branded organization, it is then possible to attract the business currently owned by the competition and gain profitable market share.

The Importance of Marketing in a Health Care Company

It is imperative that all departments within a health care company recognize that the business would be inoperable without successful marketing efforts, and that individuals play a critical role in attaining marketing objectives—including all employees not in the marketing function. The ultimate measure of success for a marketing executive is the ability to establish a corporation in which individuals understand that his or her job has a direct impact on whether the customer buys a product, and accordingly completes each task with an eye toward remaining aligned with marketing objectives and satisfying both internal and external customer needs.

It is particularly difficult to unite large corporations in their marketing efforts, as the disparities between the cultures within such international corporations may be significant, particularly in organizations that have grown as a result of a series of acquisitions. In order to facilitate consistency between marketing departments in large multi-national organizations, it is helpful to establish parameters dictating the expectations and requirements of marketing personnel throughout the company.

To aid in defining such parameters, systems have been established through which it is now possible to measure the competency levels of employees working in sales and marketing within the organization globally. While these tools do not necessarily measure performance (this is covered by a separate people performance management tool), it does provide an accurate gauge of individual leadership capabilities and marketing competencies. In this way, the company is better able to determine which development programs may be most beneficial to employees to ultimately ensure that all marketing professionals within the organization approach marketing efforts with a common ideology.

Motivating the Marketing Team

Departmental goals are essentially determined by the strategic direction of the business. The company's direction and mission should be delineated in simple, easy-to-communicate terms that are easily understood by everyone in the organization, ensuring that all individuals are working toward a common goal. To ensure that all employees and departments remain aligned with company objectives, it is advisable to schedule regular departmental meetings to determine how much progress has been made to date and to reestablish the methods by which short- and long-term company objectives may be attained.

Individuals within the department should recognize the impact their actions have on the company's success, as this is the surest way to motivate employees to continue to succeed. To this end, feedback should be provided, for example, upon receipt of annual market reports and regularly on the business's quarterly financial goals and achievements in the market, share growth, and so on, but with end customer examples of how we have made a difference in helping our customers deliver quality health care. This reinforces the value the company places on its workforce. Managers are also compensated on performance bonus targets, but more importantly by obtaining satisfaction in seeing the products and solutions used with our customers and their patients all over the globe.

The Value of Knowing the Customer

To be successful in the highly competitive health care industry, it is imperative for marketing executives to remain in contact with the sales force and the company's customers. For example, at Philips Medical Systems, the marketing team conducts several major global product introduction trainings annually. During these trainings, individual product managers, segment managers, and their counterparts in marketing and communications are responsible for training the company's worldwide sales organization in any new products coming to market. When traveling for these trainings, which may be conducted in the United States, Central Europe, China, or Japan, executives are expected to do extensive research on the business dynamics of the area, interact with customers, and determine how the company may best meet the needs of those customers in the future. In this way, when executives return to the home office, there is a comprehensive understanding of the global company, its customers, and the market, that extends far beyond simple rhetorical knowledge.

The Shifting Perception of Marketing in Health Care

Today, there is a greater appreciation of the role marketing plays in the health care industry than ever before. In the past, many decisions as to what products and technologies should be developed were based upon the recommendations of research and development, with less time or expense devoted to conducting adequate market research. Rather than being led by technological developments and capabilities, health care companies are beginning to recognize that our end user customers rarely purchase a product merely because it is technologically advanced; there must be a true compelling need for the product, which is most often determined by conducting a comprehensive analysis of the market. Today, the priority is on providing new technologies that improve safety, improve patient outcomes, and increase productivity for the health care provider, thus reducing costs. If the products or solutions being considered do not meet these requirements, there is little chance of success in the marketplace.

The rules of engagement with respect to the marketing side of health care are becoming more complex due largely to the increased number of mandated requirements for hospital technologies. As a result, hospitals will be looking for tools that will demonstrably improve their levels of compliance to protocols they are increasingly having to adhere to in various care settings, thus improving their patient outcomes. This will affect marketing in health care companies by necessitating that marketing professionals have knowledge of the various governmental requirements, standards organizations, and quality organizations across the country and around the world. To accommodate these varying requirements, health care companies must have the ability to cost-effectively adapt their technologies and solutions to fit the compliance needs of specific care settings or hospitals. These solutions from Philips Medical Systems will offer direct clinical decision support to our health care delivery clinician customers such that the products and solutions they purchase from us will directly and positively impact safety, outcomes, productivity, and reduce the cost of care delivery while maintaining or improving the quality of care delivered.

As a result of the increased need for networking and wireless technologies, the profile of the marketing professional in health care has changed significantly in the past five to six years. Today, this individual must have knowledge extending beyond marketing and the health care industry to the specific technologies required for the company to be competitive. In an ever-evolving industry, today's health care technology vice president of marketing must have a comprehensive understanding of the multitude of regulations governing the industry, an aptitude for reading and anticipating market trends, sufficient technological knowledge to direct research and development into the future, and the ability to coordinate the marketing efforts of the company on a global scale.

David A. Russell is vice president of global marketing for patient monitoring (executive level) at Philips Medical Systems. Prior to accepting this role, he was worldwide marketing manager for patient monitoring with Agilent Technologies' health care solutions group. (Philips Medical Systems acquired Agilent's health care solutions group in 2001.)

He is responsible for managing patient monitoring's global marketing initiatives, which include overall product solution portfolio management, worldwide outbound marketing communication, and business development across the three primary market segments: critical and cardiac care, anaesthesia care, and perinatal care. Mr Russell is currently based in Boeblingen, Germany, at the Philips Medical Systems Boeblingen GmbH facility, and from 2002 to 2005 he was based at the Philips Medical Systems headquarters in Andover, Massachusetts.

Since joining Hewlett Packard's medical products group in 1980 (Agilent Technologies began operating on November 1, 1999 as a result of Hewlett Packard's decision to create two independent companies from the existing Hewlett-Packard), Mr. Russell has held a variety of management positions including perinatal marketing manager, product marketing manager, and critical care marketing manager, all in the area of patient monitoring, as well as managing director of Philips Medical Systems Boeblingen GmbH .

He has a B.Sc. honors degree in electrical and electronic engineering from the University of Leeds in England and is a chartered engineer of the Institution of Electrical Engineers.

Rising to the Many Challenges of Health Care Marketing

Shawn P. Fojtik

Chief Executive Officer

Pinyons Medical Technology Inc.

Ethical Goals and Patient Centricity

Health care marketing is unique because it requires the consideration of various components that are perhaps not actively considered in other marketing industries. Working in the health care field, however, the marketing professional must consider clinical needs of the present, anticipate the needs of the future, ensure the technology's concordance with global regulations, fend off multinational competitors, and, most importantly, put patient care and safety above all else. It is not enough to have a profitable product; in making products safe, we need to anticipate a wide statistical range of users and applications, including product misuse and off-label use. Anticipating procedural problems and mitigating them with product design improvements instead of product use warnings should be a goal of all involved in the health care industry.

John Abele, co-founder of Boston Scientific, would constantly remind the sales and marketing team that there's no such thing as a simple procedure. Every patient is someone's father or mother, brother or sister, son or daughter, and those in the health care industry need to act at all times with that in mind. The greatest accolades we receive as sales and marketing leaders at Boston Scientific are letters from physicians to our senior management in recognition of a representative who went above and beyond the call of duty to serve patients.

My first exposure to patient centricity at Boston Scientific was during the interview process when I accompanied a Chicago sales representative into the field. We were watching a case to therapeutically embolize a gastro intestinal bleed. The physician was using our wires but did not have a catheter that could follow the wire. The representative I was with knew of a catheter made by a competitor that could follow the wire, but the hospital we were at did not stock this product. So, the representative got in his car, drove to the neighboring hospital, borrowed the catheter from their inventory, and drove back to the gastro intestinal bleed case in time to have the catheter used to complete the case. For me, this example epitomizes the Boston Scientific devotion to patient care. We would rather use a competitor's product, if it was needed to safely complete a case, than put the patient at risk to make a sale.

More companies should adopt a patient-centric attitude, recognizing that the health care industry has an obligation beyond the profit margin to serve patient needs. If companies stay true to a patient-centered mantra and commercialize value-added products at fair market price, the endeavor should yield sustainable profit. Besides, at the end of the day, helping patients is hopefully one of the reasons we get into health care marketing.

Part of achieving patient-centered policies is meeting the spirit of the law rather than just the letter. Months after launching a new delivery system for the Greenfield Vena Cava Filter, we began receiving complaints about the filter not releasing fully from the delivery system to deploy inside the patient's body. Our first obligation was to ensure that the complaints, perceived or real, would not pose a patient safety issue. After completing a risk analysis on the situation, we could not identify a situation where an undeployed filter stuck in our delivery system would present a patient risk. The number of reports were very small, and many of the investigations found that the filter was deploying, but sometimes it was deploying in the wrong place due to anatomical variance or physician error. A very small number of cases suggested that our protective capsule led to a situation where the filter may not fully deploy if the delivery system was excessively bent due to anatomy or physician technique. Our analysis further concluded that we were far from having to worry about a Food and Drug Administration warning letter or recommended recall. But, to meet the spirit of our commitment to patients, our customers, and regulatory agencies, we reduced the capsule length and initiated a full voluntary market recall. Patients, patient families, and physicians trust our products, and we should be worthy of that trust.

Gaining the Marketing Edge: Perpetual Learning and Teaching

When a health care company is known for patient-centric policies and care, its reputation itself will be an excellent marketing tool. However, there are other factors that can give a company the edge on its competitors.

One significant way in which marketers can gain an advantage is embracing product, procedural, and "knowledge" gaps. Most marketers know more about their products than their customers. Few computer consumers, for example, know more than a Dell product manager about the components and use of a home computer. Even if the Dell marketing leader commissions new market research, they do so knowing much more about the market and user habits than those they will survey.

In the health care industry, however, marketers go to work every day knowing that their clinical customers can have a better command of the marketer's product and procedure than they do. Instead of being intimidated by this knowledge gap, marketers should see it as a chance to learn about new opportunities. Each time a marketer meets with a clinician, he or she should seize the chance to gather data and share it with their team. Clinical observations are the marketer's chance to go back to school, learn, and then teach their team.

That said, clinical customers don't know everything. Most clinicians learned from a combination of textbook information and on-the-job training. The "see one, do one, and teach one" cliché of medical training is grounded in real-life fact. Such education can pass down tribal knowledge with product or procedural biases or overlook areas that are, at the time, relatively minor. The way a clinician learns angioplasty balloon inflation in one university may be different from the way it is taught in another across town.

Marketers cannot assume customers know everything about their products, their competitors' products, or the procedures involved. We cannot demand that our customers connect the dots between market need and product solutions. When we lead with product solutions and feature-benefit selling, we run the risk of sounding like a typical salesperson trying to schlep their wares. It is therefore important that marketers possess sound technical, clinical, and product knowledge and be able to articulate it.

Embrace the Rules of Engagement: Global Regulatory and Reimbursement

Health care marketers must also understand the global regulatory environment in which their products will be used. Getting a Class II product to market is different in the United States, Japan, and Europe, and the savvy marketer will embrace these changes. Neophyte marketers look at regulatory agencies as barriers and roadblocks, but progressive leaders see opportunities to increase quality and care among the entire industry. If we all play by the same rules, we even the playing field and ensure a fair game.

Along these lines, it's crucial that marketers understand and anticipate the reimbursement environment. Physicians, nurses, and technologists rarely, if ever, pay for medical products. Instead, hospitals pay for devices and pass the costs onto the patients' insurance or the government. Marketers must know if their products are covered by existing reimbursement or if they must go and get a new reimbursement code assigned.

The "old-school" way of approaching reimbursement had two approaches, develop and launch a product then:

1. Use existing codes that apply to your product and procedure.
2. Apply for a special reimbursement through the U.S. Department of Health and Human Services (now known as the Centers for Medicare and Medicaid Services) after the product launches.

Old School Reimbursement Afterthought

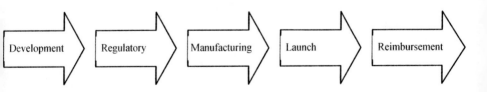

Using an existing code is acceptable if, and only if, your new product and procedure is exactly like the previous product and procedure for which the code was designed. Marketers absolutely do not want to stretch the interpretation of reimbursement codes to apply to their products. Loosely expanding codes onto products can open up the company and employees to charges of fraud. Third-party legal advice from a coding expert is mandatory when creating a coding strategy. When in doubt, do not advise customers on coding matters.

If no existing code is available, the old-school approach typically resulted in companies applying for reimbursement after the product was launched. Companies then used post-launch market data to lobby the Centers for Medicare and Medicaid Services for new reimbursements.

Concurrent Reimbursement Approach

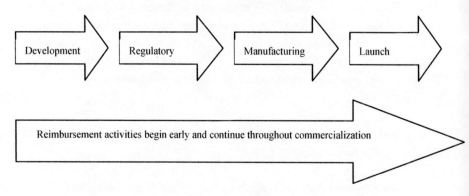

The "concurrent" reimbursement approach differs from the old-school approach in one major way: Reimbursement activities are started during product development and continue throughout commercialization. In the best case scenario, the regulatory study used to validate regulatory testing is used in part to justify a new code. The best first example of concurrent reimbursement strategy is Johnson & Johnson's Cordis Cardiovascular's work to get the Drug Eluting Stent approved with a new reimbursement code at the same time as their Food and Drug Administration approval.

How Marketing Can Help

As the chief marketing officer (CMO) of Pinyons Medical Technology, I strive to achieve speed, simplicity, and innovation to market with a safe, effective medical device in a niche other companies have neglected or underdeveloped. Strategically, we look to solve problems the physician, nurse, technologist, and other medical professionals don't even know they have. Looking for unvoiced problems forces us to be masters of procedures and the environments where our products are used. By ensuring speed, simplicity, and innovation, the marketing department can help make Pinyons a stable, profitable company.

Crediting Jack Welch and General Electric for introducing us to a speed, simplicity, and self-confidence vision of working, in medical device marketing we replace self-confidence with innovation. Innovation is a key to driving new product development, gaining a competitive edge, and improving patient care. Adding innovation also recognizes that innovation needs to be included in the marketer's personal goals for adding shareholder value.

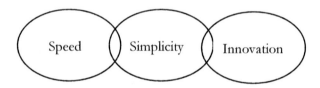

Speed

Medical devices take time to develop and commercialize. Products must be specified. Specifications must be validated. Testing regiments must be identified, then validated. No matter how good a product is, there is always room to make it better. No matter how safe a product is, there is almost always a way to make it safer. There are more than enough distractions to delay product commercialization; marketers must drive speed into decision-making at all levels of the organization.

In product development, marketers can increase the speed of a project by creating a succinct product or a marketing specification for the team to work with. Often, product specifications drift and change as development matures. The more the marketer can educate engineers about the environment in which their products are used, the faster the product can develop. Earlier, we described how we cannot assume clinicians know all the answers; here, too, we cannot assume our engineering team has all the clinical knowledge needed for commercialization.

One helpful practice I used to educate our engineering team was to hold a monthly in-service to educate our development engineers. We started with overviews of the market and procedures one week, then graduated up to discussing complex case reviews, or morbidity sessions, to show how clinicians solved complex cases. Education plus setting succinct specifications are powerful for driving speed into project completion.

Simplicity

We market complex medical devices to educated decision-makers. Marketers need to constantly simplify products and communication methods to get the strongest, most useful points across to our users. Devices used in procedures need to accommodate a wide range of potential clinical users and regions. Avoiding needless complexity lets our sales force emphasize needed information and allows our customers to get more use from our products.

Adding simplicity starts in product development. Marketers need to educate the development team about the wide range of users in the clinical marketplace. A physician in an affluent Chicago suburban hospital likely has a much different surgical environment than a physician at Chicago's Cook County Hospital. From a global marketing perspective, the differences become even larger.

At GE OEC, our engineering team understood the need for simplicity. The Series 9800 system was designed to boot up into an advanced procedure ready mode allowing physicians to press one button and image. We did not want to rely on the physician or technologist to possess the knowledge of how to make the system work. Bluntly, we wanted a "dummy-proof" system. Advanced imaging, like angiography, required a bit more training, but after a few demonstrations the system was easily learned by most users.

By comparison, Philips launched their BV300 imaging system about the same time we launched ours. Their system also booted into an imaging mode, but the user had to page through a few screens to get to advanced imaging. Angiography required more user interface and training.

In marketing, GE OEC and Philips collateral marketing materials had technical data. Philips' technical data was complemented by narrative on the types of cases that could be performed with their system, but GE OEC's copy described specific clinical challenges and how our technology would help improve outcomes. GE OEC copy was complemented with technical question-and-answer in the margin to educate and simplify the technical jargon.

We did not assume a surgeon was trained in X-ray physics and understood the difference between a .3 and .6 focal spot, or a rotating and fixed anode X-ray tube, or a computer frame grabber and a cinematic fifteen- to thirty-frame-per-second frame grabber matched to a fifteen- to thirty-frame-per-second pulsed generator. Our marketing efforts to simplify and educate teamed with focused sales execution gave GE OEC a six to one sales advantage over Philips.

Innovation

Finally, successful health care marketers recognize that research and development teams and physicians do not have a lock on medical device innovation. Marketing needs to set department goals and contribute to intellectual property development. As later discussed, medical device marketers need to be in the field, among product users and the sales force, to understand where the market is and where it is going. We then need to enthusiastically share our experience with engineers, technicians, assemblers, general management, and other marketers to create offensive and defensive intellectual property.

Creating intellectual property, or "inventing," is not as difficult as it seems. Knowing the environment where products are used, being able to identify current and future problems, and then applying common sense solutions are the mothers of innovation. The more time marketers spend in the field, the more they will be able to anticipate needs and innovate for the future.

Being an Effective CMO: Embrace Evolution and Future Vision

There is nothing more telling of a medical device marketer's metal than the way they seek out and evaluate new ideas or products. In "Marketing 101," we are taught that marketing involves meeting customer needs. In later marketing research classes, we learn that going to the market, asking what customers need, and tailoring products to meet needs is a classic product planning. Following a classic "Marketing 101" pathway of asking the market what it needs, meeting the need, and then delivering the need is only part of what it takes to be a successful medical device marketer. Medical device marketers must see what can be in the future and take risks on the products needed to get there.

In 1986, you would have had a hard time finding an engineering team or physician to articulate the need for a coronary stent. Coronary arterial bypass surgery was effective; single-digit percentage morbidity and mortality was accepted, and long recovery times were considered part of healing. Balloon angioplasty devices were in their infancy, and cardiovascular surgeons downplayed the potential for less invasive solutions of the future.

Ten years later, in 1996, balloon angioplasty was a high-growth market and coronary bypass surgeries were rapidly declining. Another ten years later, in 2006, the global coronary procedural stent market is four times larger than open heart surgery. Imagine how much faster stents would have taken off if the concept of adding mechanical scaffolding, or stents, to balloon angioplasty was envisioned by a marketing person in 1986.

Likewise, in 1992, there weren't a lot of companies that wanted to devote resources to a $250-per-case percutaneous arterial closure device. The concept of closing an arterial access site faster with more certainty was not discussed. In 2006, the closure device market will exceed $1 billion.

When ideas enter an organization, ineffective marketers usually go to their internal team and possibly to their key clinicians to get opinions. The presentation usually demonstrates or explains technology and then asks what the team or clinician thinks. Most commonly, the response is that customers aren't asking for the newly proposed products.

Market sensing and asking customers for what they need is part of classic marketing, but disruptive change comes from those who see what the market is today, then see what the market will need tomorrow. Wayne Gretsky's famous (paraphrased) "I don't go to where the hockey puck is, I go to where it is going" best articulates this concept. Consumer marketing shares this goal. No one in 1992 was asking for a $4 cup of coffee, but now we trip over a new Starbucks store as we walk the urban streets in most developed counties. In 1982, no housewife was asking for a 5,000-pound, four-wheel-drive SUV with nine inches of ground clearance to drive the kids to soccer. Developing products ahead of customer demand separates marketing "science" from "art" and will continue to define the great contributions to improvements in patient care.

The downside is that predicting the future is difficult. Many predictions about the future are wrong. We can waste millions chasing "art" while we miss the chance to "scientifically" grow in increments. The best marketers know how to effectively balance the two.

Leadership Qualities: Include Field Inputs to Strategic Plans

Successful medical device market leaders are intelligent, infectiously enthusiastic, innovative, and willing to learn from talent in the field. Such people thrive on learning and eagerly share new knowledge with their teams. There is something to learn from everyone, whether sales representatives, engineers, or clinicians. Field sales bias, customer intimacy, and the ability to overestimate competitors also contribute to success as a CMO.

Most organizations use their sales leaders to create tactical programs. Few organizations participate in strategic activities, including product innovation and product development. Even fewer attempt to educate their sales talent to participate in strategic activities. Much of this resistance is well founded: Distracting sales talent from current tactical challenges can lead to lost sales, while sales reps too involved in future product design can delay closing sales for their current product. Marketers must govern how much they disclose, and to whom, while maximizing the amount of time they spend face to face with sales team members and customers.

Spending time with a variety of customers is also key to identifying trends, gathering competitive information, and driving innovation. Most of the time, when health care marketers go in the field, they tend to gravitate toward high-profile clinicians. Early adopter clinicians should be part of the CMO's field rolodex, but a successful CMO needs to spend equal time with clinicians who support competitive products and those who perform a lot of procedures but are not necessarily "high-profile."

At General Electric's GE OEC Medical Systems, our marketing teams understood the value of calling on all clinician types. If the account was a "Siemens" or "Philips" shop, we still focused on them for tactical and strategic market activities. In one circumstance, we focused our efforts on a talented surgeon who reportedly owned a significant share of a niche competitor. We knew our chances of winning his transactional business were low, but we took it as an opportunity to learn why his lab favored the competitive system and what we could do to improve our platform. Last time I checked, GE OEC still maintains a relationship with this surgeon.

Value and Drive Field Sales Talent

Few health care products can be sold via mass commercial marketing. Even pharmaceutical companies with multimillion-dollar advertising, including national television ads, employ hundreds of professional sales representatives to meet face to face with clinicians. These sales professionals meet with clinicians to detail products, provide training, give technical advice, and fend off competitive advances.

Marketers need to understand that direct selling competencies can make or break a product, and we must build sales force repeatability into every marketing plan. If you want the customer to remember four key features of your product, you must communicate the features to the sales force in a way that allows them to quickly learn and repeat the message. If you want your sales team to use third-party, peer-reviewed clinical papers to validate product claims, you must train your team on the clinical papers.

For example, tactically, at the field sales level, we see procedural biases all the time with clinicians unaware of new product solutions. A physician on one side of town may automatically pull a soft, pre-shaped hydrophilic coated guide wire and take three minutes to cross a difficult lesion. On the other side of town, another physician performing a similar procedure may pull a comparatively stiff user-shapeable hydrophobic coated wire and take ten minutes to cross a similar lesion. The physician that takes ten minutes rarely gets to work with other physicians, and they may not know there is an alternative out there to cut their procedure time.

This ten-minute physician may not know that ten minutes is three times as long as necessary to do the same work, because they have no frame of reference. An inexperienced marketer or sales professional may approach the ten-minute physician and say they have a device to save time in crossing lesions. This approach rarely works, as the need for speed in this example has not been established.

Rather, the marketer must be able to discuss the clinical situation, describe or get the clinician to describe the problem, discuss the implication of the problem, and then present the solution. Ideally executed, the marketer establishes the need and clinically discusses what it takes to cross a difficult lesion before they even suggest a product solution.

The situation, problem, implication, and need or solution technique of selling is well described in Neil Rackman's SPIN selling model. The SPIN acronym can conger negative connotations and implies hiding or spinning the truth. But the SPIN technique should deliver the opposite, as it forces us to understand the real clinical needs for products and then allows us to present the needs with fact-based accuracy and truth. Tactically and strategically, SPIN can open up new selling and marketing opportunities while it disciplines us to master our markets, the problems our customers experience, and our product solutions.

SPIN Tactical Selling Example

SITUATION: "Doctor, I see this patient has a concentric plaque in the proximal left iliac. It looks like wire wants to advance medial as it crosses over the aortic bifurcation." We establish the situation focus and common procedure.

PROBLEM: "The wire appears to bounce off the plaque each time it is advanced. I also notice the wire was pulled out two or three times to reshape it. The wire looks kinked." Successful problem discussion forces us to identify problems the customer does not know they have.

IMPLICATION: "What happens when the wire kinks? What happens if a stiff wire breaks off a piece of plaque?" Successful implication discussions require command of the failure mode of competitive products or procedures.

Applying SPIN to tactical marketing and collateral marketing material can be a valuable team development tool. Every time we communicate a feature of our products or services to our sales team, we should do so in a way that gives an overview of the clinical situation, describes problems and the events the problems create, and then suggests a need and product solution. The alternative to SPIN is a traditional feature/benefit or feature/advantage/benefit communication model. Feature benefit selling has a place, but it does not discipline us to master disease state, procedural, or competitive environments. SPIN techniques should be built into collateral marketing when writing copy for product brochures.

Classic Feature and Benefit Copy

GE OEC's Series 9800 Vascular Imaging System

The new GE OEC Series 9800 imaging system is a major advance in mobile intraoperative imaging. The Series 9800 features 1,000 line by 1,000 line, or 1,000,000 pixels, providing the highest image resolution in its class. GE OEC's proprietary imaging chain and high-powered generator makes 1,000 x 1,000 line resolution possible to increase image detail during complex procedures. Combined with 1,000 line imaging is GE OEC's 60-watt high-power X-ray generator. A high-powered generator provides benefit of added power when needed to penetrate dense anatomy and further increase image quality. Finally, the Series 9800 is the first mobile imaging system to include AutoTrak anti-blooming software. AutoTrak helps preserve the image quality when the X-ray tube or patient anatomy is not centered on the screen when imaging. AutoTrak is a benefit, as it prevents "wash out" and resetting the X-ray settings each time the patient anatomy is off-center near the edge of the screen.

Feature	Benefit & Advantage
1,000 x 1,000 line resolution visualization of anatomy	Increased image quality for better
AutoTrak	Anti-blooming software to prevent over exposure and image "wash-out."

Solution-Based SPIN Copy

GE OEC Series 9800 Vascular Imaging System

Endovascular abdominal aortic aneurysm ("AAA") placement is a demanding procedure. The AAA graphs must be sized precisely to the native proximal and distal aorta, place accurately beneath the renal arteries via fluoroscopic guidance and imaged post-placement to ensure placement accuracy and that there are no endoleaks. Placing the AAA too high over a renal can shut down blood supply to a kidney or contribute to hypertension. Missing an endoleak can cause the graph to migrate, prolapse upon itself, or put the patient at risk of AAA rupture.

Surgeons need an imaging system to help ensure AAA graph placement accuracy and rule out endoleaks. The Series 9800 Vascular Image System meets the need for increased image quality with the industry's first and only 1,000 line by 1,000 line resolution. $1,000^2$ image resolution means 1 million pixels of resolution to better visualize graph placement accuracy and discrete endoleaks.

Solution-based selling matched to solution-based collateral marketing materials will make communication consistent throughout the organization. Every marketing brochure and sales meeting should be not only an attempt to sell technology but also an opportunity for participants to come away with increased knowledge about procedures and/or disease states. When clinicians, sales representatives, and marketers are well informed, the entire industry benefits.

Overestimate Competition

Finally, CMOs should overestimate the competition. For example, when I inherited Boston Scientific's 46,500-unit, $50 million Vena Cava Filter business in 1997, I was surprised to see how cavalierly we treated our competitors. The previous Vena Cava Filter marketing leaders discounted our competitors' market success and characterized us to senior management as the overwhelming market driving an overall 5 percent market growth rate. They did not market segment or fully investigate our competitor's position. In addition, they only used one third-party source to validate their market shares.

Specifically, the previous Boston Scientific Vena Cava Filter managers subscribed to a third-party research group that sampled hospital purchase orders to estimate market shares. Based on this data, the third-party research organization reported Boston Scientific's Vena Cava Filter market share as 71 percent of Vena Cava Filter units and 75 percent of profits. This same study estimated the total market for Vena Cava Filters growing at 11 percent with 90,900 units and $90 million in sales. Past management accepted in full the report's unit and market share estimates but discounted the growth, units, and market size without footnoting this data to senior management.

We knew our sales were growing at 5 percent with 46,500 units and $50 million sold. If the market was 90,900 units and $90 million, our share was actually 51 percent of units and 56 percent of profits. Worse, if the market was growing at 11 percent and we were growing at 5 percent, we were losing share. To be sure, I investigated the published sales revenue from a competitor as reported in Securities and Exchange Commission documents and found that we were dramatically underestimating their market share. A small field sales force survey uncovered equally high penetration by our competitors, particularly in interventional radiologists.

By triangulating the data between numerous sources, I determined that we had been overestimating our share by as much as twenty points and we were quickly losing share in the high-growth interventional radiology space of our market. The new data helped us justify increased resource allocation toward developing our new low-profile Vena Cava Filter, designed to meet the needs of interventional radiologists.

The market share data triangulation exercise was valuable, but it would have been better if previous management was vigilant about overestimating competitors from the start. By underestimating competitors, we lost share and gave competitors valuable space in high-growth interventional radiology.

One of my first lessons in marketing was that we can define our market share any way we want if we decide what the "market" is. Rolls Royce automobiles have a high market share when we define the market as British Luxury cars over $200,000. The Ford Taurus sedan seems to have a reasonable market share when we define the market as new sedans sold. However, if you take the rental car company purchases out, their share drops dramatically. We make different business decisions depending on whether we are a market leader in a stable market or a market newcomer in a high-growth space. We also need to question our market share sources for accuracy and triangulate data against two, three, or four sources whenever possible.

Working with Other Executives

Marketing is one part of an effective, integrated company. The CMO works most closely with the chief executive officer (CEO) and leaders of sales and research and development. Teamwork with each involves a different approach in order to get the most from the relationship.

The CEO and CMO must communicate fluently with each other about the company's strategic plan, tactical plan, and day-to-day results. CMOs must understand that CEOs touch all departments, plus the board or shareholder representative, and must coordinate all of them with the company's broader vision.

The CMO can use their knowledge of the CEO's responsibilities by communicating their activities in a way that speaks to the CEO's areas of responsibility. CMOs should be able to describe their operations to the CEO at all times in terms of how they relate to the whole company: "When we execute this marketing initiative, here is how it effects (insert department name)." Many CMOs earn the number-two position in the company behind the CEO to give the board an internal succession plan for the current CEO.

The CMO must be equally close with the sales leadership to help motivate tactical success and stay close to the customer. A CMO's work with the sales leader can ensure that new collateral marketing material educates customers and trains representatives. He or she can also help the sales leader create field sales incentive programs that are consistent with the strategic plan for future growth. Aligning the marketing tactics with sales tactics is mandatory. Marketing should be prepared to lead, and simultaneously be subordinate, to current customer and sales activity. CMOs lead by setting the vision and strategy for the department, and they are subordinate as they should go to work every day with a willingness to learn from sales.

Research and development leadership is another key executive to work closely with. As previously described, CMOs must take ownership for product innovation that serves the strategic plan. By coordinating the research and development team with opinions from key clinical opinion leaders, CMOs can create smart in-field product differentiation tools based on basic science and engineering in which a sales or marketing executive may not be trained.

Managing a Team and a Budget

Patient centricity, goal orientation, intelligence, innovation, and mission-critical problem-solving skills are the most important skills for a marketing leader. We can take a risk on less tenured candidates if they demonstrate these attributes. Someone can gain experience and learn from colleagues, but it's much harder to develop the personal qualities we value.

Similar to a classic organization chart, team goals are a direct subset of the company's strategic plan, which should focus the company on three to five areas to improve. A CMO should take the company focus areas, simplify them one step further, and have three to four areas for the entire marketing and sales team to build their goals in. The team goals should then distil down to individual goals, and all objectives should be coordinated with the strategic plans. On a quarterly basis, the team can formally review progress, making sure the company is where it wants to be and, if it isn't, determining how to get there.

The marketing team should also be aware of the department budget and efforts to control expense. Personnel costs are usually the top line of the marketing team's expenses. But, scrubbing salary, bonus, or long-term equity expenses are the last place a marketing leader should go to scrub the budget.

It costs more to replace or hire back an employee with counteroffers than it does to pay an existing one well from the beginning. Ideally, it is best to spend money on performance-driven mid- and long-term compensation as opposed to high base pay. High base pay becomes an annuity to be increased most every year, while variable mid- and long-term compensation can grow or stabilize with the business. In the end, the little more we give in compensation to an individual means much more to those receiving it as opposed to us in giving it.

Overpaid talent is only overpaid if we do not take it upon ourselves to put into action plans to get the most out of our employees. Most team members need to be led to achieve their full potential. Under-leading and overpaying talent is not the employee's fault; it is the fault of the manager and incumbent.

Trade shows, advertising and promotion, and travel are the largest expenses outside of team talent costs. Trade show presence is an important venue for medical device marketing. Properly executed, a medical device trade show can be a powerful event to reinforce existing customers, reach new customers, meet with vendors, monitor competitive activity, and energize your team. But trade shows are expensive, and many companies overspend in an attempt to create a presence or "keep up with the Joneses."

Trade show booths usually do not have to be as large as they are and present a chance to save money. It is difficult to qualify the difference between a twenty-by-twenty booth, or 400 square feet at $30 per foot for a total of $12,000, and a thirty-by-thirty booth, or 900 square feet at $30 per foot for a total of $27,000. Still, you can find thirty-by-thirty booths at every meeting with few clinician customers taking up the space.

Advertising and promotion is another area in which to spend carefully. Many companies spend a lot of their budget sponsoring events at trade shows or physician symposiums. Sponsoring can be effective, but too often we see companies signing up for sponsorships and then not getting the full mileage out of the event. What has more impact, if "St. Jude" sponsors the morning speaker session at a heart association meeting or if the new "Victory Pacemaker by St. Jude" sponsors the session. In general, better targeting and focus is needed when companies spend their precious promotional dollars. In the end, when managing big budgets, the question can come down to: "Do we do this major promotion or trade show schedule, or do we take that money and put another sales professional on the street?"

Creating a Strategic Plan

Reaching company goals requires consistent planning. My primary strategy recommendation for CMOs is to create a living strategic plan and schedule time to formally visit various sections, review progress, critique, and plan for the future. Cadence and process is important as team size grows. The military figured this out a long time ago; teams that march the same way have an easier time taking on new projects, or orders, as opposed to those that march to different beats. This, of course, is not to say we need to conform in the way we innovate or interact with each other. Many practices in business are broken and need to be fixed, but fixing them with a common methodology helps us add new ideas to the team without skipping a beat.

The strategic plan should start with a complete product and market review. Where are we? Where is the market? Where is it going? High-level gap analysis and candid core competency review are musts for this stage. Our plan needs to start with detailed product analysis backed by third-party and internal market validation, graduate to candid internal competencies and capabilities, then result in a working plan.

The General Electric strategic planning process is a great template for success. Without getting into a "chicken or the egg" argument, our strategic plan at GE OEC opened in October with delivery of the World Wide Product Plan (WWPP).

Season One, October WWPP: The WWPP investigated our position in each market, analyzed competitive strengths and weakness, speculated the direction of the market, and suggested actions for leadership. In short, "who are we, who are they (competition), and where this thing is going." Speculation on the future should include conservative predictions with "What if?" ideas on how to disruptively change the market. Obviously, delivering the WWPP in early October meant we needed to continually work on the WWPP deliverables throughout the year.

<u>Season Two, January Strategic Plan Part 1 ("S1")</u>: The CEO's executive team must take inputs from the WWPP to sign up for a plan for the future. "Are we going to maintain what we have and grow with the market through internally driven disruptive market change?" Alternatively, "We will drive to increased profitability through vertical integration and commit to controlling all aspects of product commercialization." Last, "We are going to grow through acquisition." S1 must put together the vision for the coming year and decade ahead. It becomes the "who we want to be and how to get there" plan.

<u>Season Three, April Team Plan ("Team")</u>: GE did a great job of managing talent. Creating a great plan without scoping the talent to execute was a miss. Talent needs to formally be reviewed as an executive team. During the Team season of the strategic plan, the "one-up" manager reviewed the "two-down" team members to understand accomplishments, opportunity areas, and career goals. For example, a CEO, or one-up, would review the employee evaluation of the direct reports of their direct reports, or two-down. CEOs gained direct exposure to a CMO's upstream and downstream marketing managers. CMOs then gained exposure to their marketing manager's product and marketing communication team. It sounds intuitive, but it is amazing how many companies turn this process into a rubber stamp as opposed to a formal review and development process.

<u>Season Four, July Strategic Plan II ("S2")</u>: S2 is a simple six-month return to the Strategic Plan, or S1, delivered in January. S2 takes into account a midyear review of how the plan is rolling out and what needs to change to make the year.

Throughout the Strategic Plan process, marketing should lead the communication of the plan to the company. Too often, companies come up with good plans but then keep the plan tight within a small operating group. The plan should have communication elements to share with every level of the company.

For example, Boston Scientific did an excellent job communicating their strategic plan with field sales. The Boston Scientific sales team would meet in February, July, and October every year to train, refocus, and discuss the plan for the future. The meetings were not boondoggle golf or ski outings.

Rather, we used the time to learn about our current procedures with more depth, learn new procedures, and recalibrate toward a common vision.

GE's strategic planning seasons can be applied to any organization to create discipline and fixed timing to revisiting the plan.

Conclusion

Successful health marketing has special challenges in maintaining patient centricity while meeting future clinical needs and working in a highly regulated environment. There is no one key to success. Like most businesses, there must be strength in every facet of the marketing executive's domain with a continuity of strength extended throughout the organization. That said, successful health care marketers share common DNA in their ability to manage numerous variables that can affect their business. Health care marketers must thrive on learning and be willing to take risks on innovation. They should embrace the fact that every patient and clinician encounter is a chance to learn and improve. We must also look at external regulatory agencies as opportunities to improve product quality and level the playing field among competitors to ensure a fair game. Marketers must stay close to clinicians and field sales for acute access to information needed to improve tactical and strategic plans. Lastly, successful executives must continue to put patient care above all else as the common denominator when making difficult decisions about the business.

Shawn Fojtik is the founder of Pinyons Medical Technology Inc. in Park City, Utah. He is the innovator of core medical devices that are designed to improve patient care and safety during angiography and angioplasty procedures. Prior to Pinyons, Mr. Fojtik was the chief operating officer of CathEffects LLC in Sacramento, California. CathEffects products include cardiac mapping and ablation catheters to diagnose and treat cardiac arrhythmia. At Pinyons and CathEffects, Mr. Fojtik's responsibilities have included general management of product development, manufacturing, regulatory, finance, marketing, and sales.

Mr. Fojtik is a board member of Control Medical Technology LLC in Park City, Utah, a development-stage company with intellectual property for catheter steering, temperature sensing, and wiring. Mr. Fojtik also serves as a consultant to Medical CV Inc. in Minneapolis, Minnesota and TZ Medical Inc. in Portland, Oregon. Earlier in his career, Mr. Fojtik held sales, global marketing, and product development leadership positions at GE Medical Systems, Boston Scientific, and Black & Decker.

Mr. Fojtik received his B.S. in advertising from the University of Illinois in Urbana, Illinois and his M.A. from Harvard University, where he wrote a thesis on the use of vena caval filters to prevent fatal pulmonary embolism. He works as an M.B.A. student mentor at the University of Utah in Salt Lake City, Utah.

The Objectives of the Health Care Human Resources Role

Mike Rude

Vice President, Human Resources

Stryker

The Role of the HR Director

In today's health care industry, the role of the human resources (HR) director is to balance organizational profitability with effective employee engagement and a certain degree of business practicality. In order to best serve the interests of the company, he or she must ensure the highest level of expertise among employees and management, develop cost containment strategies, and manage the staff and payroll growth of the organization.

The HR professional must have the confidence necessary to develop and support professional opinions in the face of potential opposition from others within the organization. In order to do this, it is imperative to have a sound understanding of not only the business of health care in general, but how the specific company earns its profits. The individual must then determine how the employees and organizational practices affect the business goals of the company.

Setting and Achieving Goals in the Health Care Industry

In order to achieve the financial goals set by a company within the health care industry, it is imperative that the best individuals and organizational strategies are in place, as the regulatory practices of the Food and Drug Administration with respect to research and development in health care are more stringent than in other industries. This translates into a need for higher levels of regulatory clinical expertise and greater attention paid to the processes and policies surrounding product innovation.

The goals established by a health care company may include a set percentage of operating income growth, globalization of the organization, increased innovation in the field, and the development of leading professionals in the industry. The goals of a health care organization typically remain constant throughout the life of the company, while the strategies and initiatives implemented to reach these goals will often change from year to year. It is advisable for a company to conduct an annual or semiannual review of any programs implemented in order to ensure that they are aligned with the long-term objectives of the organization.

Strategies for Success

In order to be successful in a health care HR leadership role, the individual must first understand the relationship between organizational practices and business objectives. For example, in order to develop the most appropriate talent acquisition and retention strategy, the HR leader needs to understand what the business strategies are regarding new markets or new products and services the company plans to develop and market so the right people with the right talents and capabilities can be sourced, recruited, hired, and any special retention plans (i.e., compensation changes, learning and development programs, special assignments) can be developed to ensure that the right people stay engaged and committed to the company for the long term.

In order to ensure that they remain active and engaged in their leadership roles, the head of HR must develop a relationship with the managers within the company, including the chief executive officer, chief financial officer, and any group and division presidents, HR division leaders, and the board of directors. There should be an understanding of the interdependence between the roles of the physicians within the company and that of the executive team members, and an appreciation of the various demands placed on each department and individual. Time must also be spent on leadership development, succession plans, and good hiring practices, as this will better ensure that the company is comprised of the best individuals in the industry.

Challenges in HR

One of the most significant challenges in HR is ensuring that the appropriate controls and governance practices are in place without becoming overly dictatorial; an organization must strike a balance between having the flexibility necessary to perform well while simultaneously working within the bounds set by the applicable governance controls.

In today's competitive environment, it is also difficult to locate and retain the best individuals in the industry; to this end, the HR director must have the ability to cultivate connections with the primary sources from which these individuals may emerge. Additional challenges include conveying to management the relevance of HR practices and their impact on the business side of health care and remaining apprised of any regulatory and governance changes in the industry, particularly with respect to Sarbanes-Oxley.

Assembling the Team

Every effort should be made by the head of HR to identify and retain the services of the most highly qualified individuals possible. Those individuals who are outstanding in the health care industry are typically those possessing a high degree of responsibility, a strong desire to achieve, a practical nature, a sense of humor, and the ability to foster relationships with others. Additionally, today's successful health care professional will have impeccable credibility, integrity, and the ability to learn.

In order to set and achieve effective goals for the various teams within an organization, it is first necessary to review the long-term business objectives of the company and ensure that the HR strategies are aligned with those objectives. To this end, detailed and specific objectives should be established annually and reviewed on a quarterly basis in order to ensure that they remain aligned with the larger business goals of the company.

The Creation of a Corporate Culture

In order to better facilitate a prosperous, functional work environment, it is first necessary for the head of HR to understand the nature of the health care culture today, and to then be able to relate that to how the attainment of business objectives are either facilitated or hindered by this culture. Working with the chief executive officer, the HR director must determine what strategies best facilitate success for the company and then strive to create a corporate culture around those strategies.

Typically, universal characteristics that are desirous in any corporate culture are also applicable in the health care industry (i.e., providing a challenging, rewarding workplace and the maximization of individual talents and expertise). Additional qualities conducive to the creation of a successful corporate culture in health care include a strong service ethic, personal accountability, the desire for exceptional results, and an environment in which constant improvement is a primary goal.

Attracting Employees

In order to attract individuals to a health care organization, it is first necessary to look at the past performance and success of that organization, stressing the positive image the company's services and history provide. The individual interested in the health care industry often has a personal, intrinsic sense of reward for the type of work he or she is doing, because the products manufactured and services offered have an impact on people's lives. Because of this, health care professionals are most often attracted to organizations with an exceptional history of success.

While a health care background is desirous in regulatory, sales, and marketing positions, other positions relating to finance, HR, or operations may not require specific health care experience. Sourcing may be done from schools or other companies to recruit the most outstanding prospects, and the utilization of various tools relating to the interview and assessment process further ensure that the company is truly selecting and retaining the best individuals in the industry. Finally, the role of the head of HR is to convince the prospect of the desirability of the company's culture and direction.

Ensuring the Retention of Qualified Employees

In order to ensure the retention of employees, the head of HR should ensure that the managers within each division are doing what is necessary to assure high levels of engagement from their employees. To this end, an engagement survey may be distributed annually, with managers held accountable for the results. Additionally, individuals should be placed in meaningful, challenging positions early in their careers, thus providing autonomy and the opportunity to gain experience and the ability to move within the company, both divisionally and geographically. While competitive wages are vital, they are ultimately not the deciding factor in determining whether an organization is able to retain its best employees for any significant period of time.

In order to inspire employees to work to their potential, it is necessary for HR to communicate the direction of the organization, ensuring that all parties have a clear understanding of the relevant priorities and objectives. Further, it is imperative that all employees remain informed as to developments within both the company and the industry in order to be competitive in their roles.

Regular company publications may be routed to all employees in order to facilitate the communication process. These publications should include the progress of the company with respect to its objectives, any ongoing key activities and initiatives, and a specific focus on various locations and divisions for each issue. Within the senior executive team, there should also be weekly meetings to update all members as to the financials and any other major organizational issues; all those in attendance should then be encouraged to disseminate any information discussed throughout the organization.

Changes in HR

In recent years, the focus of the HR director has shifted from those areas previously deemed specifically HR-related to a greater focus on understanding the business of health care. Today's HR director must demonstrate a strong understanding of the company financials and should have the ability to relate HR practices to those specific financial and strategic efforts.

Going forward, it will be imperative that HR become more global, understanding what it means to attract and retain individuals from around the world. It will become increasingly important that the HR director understand less conventional methods of hiring, whether it be part-time, contractors, or remote workers. To this end, there will be a need to become more creative with respect to methods by which talent may be identified and secured globally.

In addition, there must be a heightened understanding of governmental regulations and regulatory requirements with respect to both Sarbanes-Oxley and the Food and Drug Administration; because these regulations change frequently, it is imperative that the HR director remain current on any developments in the area. Because there is greater pressure around ethical business practices, the appropriate governance practices must be in place within today's health care organization.

Finally, while HR will always have to execute successfully on the purely administrative aspect of the job, more and more emphasis needs to be placed on delivering better business analytics. The effective HR director must have insight into how the various HR mechanisms impact the bottom line of the organization. In today's competitive world, the HR director must have the ability to demonstrate how HR adds value to the business.

Success in HR

To facilitate success in his or her role, the HR professional should be aware of any changes in the industry, tracking any developments through the *Wall Street Journal, Business Week,* and any other relevant business periodicals. Various governmental and regulatory Web sites should also be frequented in order to receive updates on upcoming conferences in the industry.

Success in HR may be gauged by the attainment of business, financial, and personal objectives within an organization. Positive responses from key constituents including the chief financial officer, chief executive officer, and division heads indicating that HR is providing good counsel and impacting recruitment are also a valuable measure of how effectively the department is performing its role in the company. Ultimately, it is imperative that the individual leading HR in the health care industry understand the business, build genuine relationships based on trust with those within the company, and fulfill any commitments made to those within the organization.

Mike Rude joined Stryker Corporation, based in Kalamazoo, Michigan, in 2000 as vice president of human resources. In this capacity, he is responsible for all worldwide human resource activities for this $4 billion, 16,000-employee orthopedic medical device manufacturer. Prior to joining Stryker, he was vice president of human resources for the Scimed division of Boston Scientific. During his four years at Boston Scientific, he was responsible for all domestic human resource activities, supervising a sixty-person human resources function for the largest fully integrated division of Boston Scientific, representing $900 million in U.S. sales and approximately 4000 employees.

Before joining Boston Scientific, Mr. Rude worked for several divisions of the Dun & Bradstreet Corporation in human resources generalist and organizational development leadership positions. He started his professional career at Baxter International, where for eight years he worked in various organizational development roles at the division, group, and corporate level.

Mr. Rude has his master's degree in organizational communication and his undergraduate degree in speech communications from the University of Illinois.

He, his wife Debbie, and three children live in Portage, Michigan.

Building a Pleasant and Productive Work Culture

Margery Ahearn

Vice President, Human Resources

Aspect Medical Systems Inc.

Goals

My goal is to provide the tools and processes to help the company build a disciplined operating culture, maintain strong bonds with our employees, and foster a vibrant and evolving company culture, retain employees, and manage growth. To do this, I've created a framework for our human resources (HR) programs that helps us link these goals together. We also focus on enabling managers and employees to communicate and understand how they help to manage the company and develop careers. Key elements of this HR system include goal setting, training, professional and leadership development, and performance management. Through this design, the organization is positioned to attract, develop, and retain high-quality employees. We try to reinforce an environment where employees feel respected, stimulated, and challenged while providing tools and processes that enhance individual and organizational effectiveness.

This vision has naturally changed over time given certain circumstances of my company. When we had approximately sixty employees, we maintained the core functional operations of HR; we focused on building a solid compensation and benefits platform, employment policies and procedures, and employment law. As the company has grown, however, we have put more emphasis on employee engagement, performance culture, and talent management. We've adopted these changes in a systematic approach that allows us to evaluate what we've done and build or change processes as necessary. We also formulate a long-range plan every year, taking stock of our current position and deciding which areas we want to enhance in the future.

For the most part, the health care industry has the same functional HR needs and demands as other high-growth areas. However, there are certain differences. As an industry, we are dedicated to continuous improvement, and therefore as a company and as part of an HR team we must also share that view for the operations of the company. We are a true business partner and believe in operational excellence and evolution of a supportive and engaged internal culture. HR is a key driver in how the culture works as well as how it is perceived. This department directly influences business issues and opportunities. This requires our HR team to be innovative, strategic, and visionary in our approach. In the health care industry and specifically the medical device industry, we require unique skill sets. We understand that to acquire these skills sets, we must invest in talent management and show a competitive advantage in people management. We strive to be considered a "company of choice" in the industry in order to attract and retain our talent base.

Influence and Strategy

The job of an HR executive is based on one's ability and effectiveness to provide an integrated HR management system that provides tools and processes to support business goals, organizational design, required competencies, succession planning, engagement initiatives, professional and leadership development programs, and training plans as well as reward design programs for performance management. Employees are considered the "customers" of HR, and part of being an HR professional is having the ability to understand their needs and align these needs with company objectives. In order to measure the success of the HR system, we develop objective and subjective methods to establish the company's benchmark with our initiatives. We are also knowledgeable on the industry and try to stay ahead of the competitive environment. We are committed to a competency approach to talent management and candidate selection, and we therefore develop and maintain programs based on our ability to attract and retain talent. These benchmarks are closely analyzed and used as the springboard for new ideas and initiatives. We continue to look for new ways to give employees the best possible opportunities and work environment. The head of HR must believe not only in the culture and vision of the business, but also in the growth and development of the employees.

As a vice president of HR, it is my responsibility to provide tools that empower the management team as well as the individual contributor. The HR department drives the creation, integration, and training of these tools and recommends the processes and the time frame for the use of these tools. If implemented correctly, these tools are fully integrated into the culture of the organization and actively drive the evolution of the culture.

The most challenging aspect I have as the head of the HR department is balancing the vision I have for the company, and more specifically the HR department itself, with the deliberate steps required in getting to that endpoint. There are times I am so full of enthusiasm to reach an outcome that I must remember to maintain the patience to go one step at a time and make sure the employees completely understand the potential results of each initiative and are appropriately involved in the design of each initiative. I want them to understand the link between our framework and the tools we produce. I resist the urge to move too quickly or add too much at one time for the purpose of understanding how each change, no matter how small, affects the operations of the company.

One tactic I use is to have an HR steering committee made up of a cross-functional cross-level group of individuals that acts as an HR board. Ideas and strategies are initially presented in this format to build understanding and an exchange that helps keep the continued development of the HR framework in focus, not only on what the HR team is trying to achieve but how we will get there. It is easy to develop tools and processes. However, it is much harder to do so in a way that clearly articulates a need and measures success.

Human Resource Framework

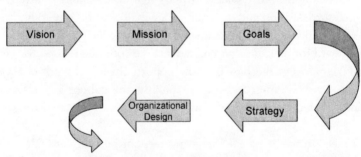

Talent Management

- Leadership Development
- Succession Planning
- Training/Development
- Recruiting
- Ind. Development Plans
- Assessments
- 360's

Relationship Culture

- Communication
- Fun
- Connection
- Benefits/Health
- Community
- Family

Performance Culture

- Goal Setting
- Performance Management
- Merit
- Market Analysis
- Bonus
- LTI Plan

HR Operations

- Records
- Compliance

Working with Executives

Because I work closely with all the executives within the company as well as the board of directors, it's important that I understand their motivations and positions on issues that arise. Much of this understanding comes with time and acquaintance; I've made an effort to learn their management styles and how they relate to one another, their teams, and to me. Having a positive working relationship with the executives is a vital part of the HR professional's job, as it improves communication and support while reducing potential issues that could arise through inadequate interdepartmental relations.

Executives can help ensure the success of HR initiatives by working closely with HR professionals and visibly supporting them. At my corporation, HR has evolved from a functional operations-only group into one that guides and shapes the relationship and performance culture with goal setting, performance management, incentives plans, talent management, and engagement activities. We work to ensure that employees have a work/life balance and are not just satisfied but truly believe Aspect Medical Systems is the "employer of choice." The executive support that the HR team has gained within the company has been vital to our success.

One example of the support our department receives is the executive team's involvement in competency modeling. Our model provides four domains: leadership, communications, decision making and judgment, and management. We define these domains for each role in the company: executive, director, manager, and individual contributor. We then assess each employee's core competencies and build an individual development plan for each member of the company, focusing on projects, mentoring, and courses that will help develop employees and executives in needed areas. We also provide tools for ongoing assessment based on these competencies and are integrating this system with the recruiting process to make sure we bring in employees who excel in these areas. Management support is vital in this system, as it makes sure the plans and training reach all employees.

In order to set goals and implement systems, the vice presidents of the company meet as an executive team and identify a number of key business objectives. Because one of those company goals is "investment in organizational development," HR receives a large amount of support as well as influence into which initiatives it should focus on for the year. This year, the objective of investing in organizational development led to several initiatives that included organizational design, competency models, on-boarding programs, enhancing internal communication, and measuring employee satisfaction. Competency modeling was a major effort that focused on talent management. This competency approach to management started with active engagement from different levels of management to build the competency model matrix. This tool is now integrated into other systems such as performance management, training and individual development plans, assessments, and recruitment. Another initiative was the on-boarding program. This program allows new employees to understand and fully engage in our culture right from their start of hire. The new hire attends a variety of informational sessions relating to different department areas over the course of four months. This comprehensive program introduces new employees to all facets of the Aspect culture in a methodical and manageable way.

Each month, the executive team meets to discuss the key business objectives and evaluate what progress has been made. Each employee has goals that roll up to functional goals that in turn roll up to these key business objectives. This type of goal setting provides a clear line of sight for the employees. Our employees understand how their objectives contribute to the overall key business objectives of the company. This line of sight system is extremely useful in ensuring clear communication among all sectors of the company.

Personal Vision

Corporate culture is created and maintained by the members of a company, from the owner or president to the entry-level employees. Once it has been created, the challenge is to maintain and enhance it by making sure new employees understand the culture and by providing programs and opportunities that keep long-term personnel aware of it. For example, in addition to technical talent, we look for leadership and flexibility in the employees we hire; by recruiting people who fit our core competencies, we're thus maintaining our corporate culture.

Our culture is one driven by performance and relationships, where people have goals to meet and performance standards to fulfill but where they can also enjoy their work and attain a balance between it and the rest of their life. This is a concept we have tried to establish from the beginning, and I don't think it's unique to the health care industry. Unless we're hiring research and development, engineering, or regulatory employees, technical medical knowledge is not the most important factor, whereas fitting into and understanding our culture is. The knowledge of the health care industry is something that can be developed over time and is applicable in different degrees to specific positions.

We are fortunate, when pursuing unique talent, that we have unique and innovative technology that receives media exposure. Events such as publicized scientific developments keep us in the public view and help us attract new employees. However, we are not necessarily in the area of the country that actively employs *some* of the talent we need. Some of the openings we actively recruit for (for example, clinical) are currently in companies that are out of state. This, at times, presents us with somewhat of a challenge. Massachusetts is an expensive state to live in, and when faced with this obstacle, potential employees often choose not to relocate. By and large, we strive to make our culture attractive enough that, despite the location, employees in all functional areas will seek us out when looking for employment.

Retaining and Inspiring Employees

Part of HR's objective is to empower employees and make sure they have a strong work/life balance. This is valuable for retention purposes. People in my company work hard and feel committed to their work because they believe that what they do will make a difference in people's lives. This attitude has spread through the company and is an asset in both maintaining corporate culture and retaining employees. Because the health care industry has this impact on others, it is sometimes easier to gain that commitment from employees as long as they clearly understand that what they do as individuals contributes to the company's mission. It is my goal to make sure that understanding exists.

Some tactics I've found useful in spreading this attitude to new employees include on-boarding, where new arrivals to the company are exposed to different aspects of our company. This helps them to understand our mission, vision, and values, as well as how we develop leadership skills. Exceptional levels of benefits, strategic compensation approaches, employee development programs, work/life programs, and engagement initiatives also let the employees know the company cares about them and is committed to being a company of choice.

Surveys and assessments are one of the main metrics HR uses to measure success. Talent management is a crucial aspect to HR; it's vital to research and address employee concerns. In addition to providing and understanding metrics, I constantly challenge myself and the rest of my department by reading available materials on employee satisfaction and corporate culture, associating with other HR professionals, and finding out which aspects of their previous HR departments worked and didn't work for their employees. All of these strategies provide feedback and innovation, which are crucial to HR success.

Changes

Historically, HR had been a tactical group, but recently the focus has shifted to strategy. We now have a welcomed seat at the table and a voice in business objectives and how a company achieves them. This is a trend I see continuing; in the coming years, I think HR professionals will be more deeply involved and have more seats not only on executive teams but on company boards as well. Metrics for HR will also expand, giving employees more feedback, and technology will become a more integral part of HR. As America turns to a more knowledge-based economy, HR will face new challenges but will also increase in importance and impact.

Advice

I find that the advice I most often give my team is to ask questions about what they're doing at the moment. Don't accept something just because it is what is most readily available to them. I challenge them to try new things, expand on their current strategies, and develop themselves, their departments, and their employees in new directions. Telling someone that his or her department has challenges or opportunities for development is comparatively easy; the real challenge is to figure out ways to push forward in a way that is productive and non-threatening.

The three golden rules of being an HR director are, first, to see all the possibilities and opportunities in a situation. There is generally more than meets the eye and more than one angle on an issue. Second, preserve your vision of the company in both the big projects and the small details. From the creation of the HR strategic framework to showing our core values in every employee presentation, believing that everything you do can make a difference represents the values of a good HR professional. Finally, retain your passion for the job. A good HR director should care about the company and be actively working to make its culture better.

Margery Ahearn is vice president of human resources. She joined Aspect Medical Systems in April of 1998 and held positions as director of staffing and, most recently, director of human resources. She has more than nineteen years of human resource experience in the medical device and high-tech industry. She held positions at GTE, CGI Inc., and Wang Laboratories before joining Aspect Medical Systems.

She holds a bachelor's degree in management and an M.B.A. from Southern New Hampshire University. She also received an advanced certificate in personnel administration/industrial relations.

Management
Best Sellers

Visit Your Local Bookseller Today or Go to www.Aspatore.com
for More Information

- Corporate Ethics - Making Sure You are in Compliance With Ethics Policies; How to Update/Develop an Ethics Plan for Your Team - $17.95
- 10 Technologies Every Executive Should Know - Executive Summaries of the Ten Most Important Technologies Shaping the Economy - $17.95
- The Board of the 21st Century - Board Members from Wal-Mart, Philip Morris, and More on Avoiding Liabilities and Achieving Success in the Boardroom - $27.95
- Inside the Minds: Leading CEOs - CEOs from Office Max, Duke Energy, and More on Management, Leadership, and Profiting in Any Economy - $27.95
- Deal Teams - Roles and Motivations of Management Team Members, Investment Bankers, Professional Services Firms, Lawyers, and More in Doing Deals (Partnerships, M&A, Equity Investments) - $27.95
- The Governance Game - What Every Board Member and Corporate Director Should Know About What Went Wrong in Corporate America and What New Responsibilities They Are Faced With - $24.95
- Smart Business Growth - Leading CEOs on Twelve Ways to Increase Revenues and Profits for Your Team/Company - $27.95

**Buy All 7 Titles Above and
Save 40% - Only $114.95**

Call 1-866-Aspatore or Visit www.Aspatore.com to Order

New Releases

- <u>HR Best Practices</u> - Top Human Resources Executives from Prudential Financial, Northrop Grumman, and More on Hiring the Right People and Enhancing Corporate Culture - $27.95
- <u>Staffing Leadership Strategies</u> - Best Practices for Working with Customers - $27.95
- <u>The Art of Consulting</u> - Gaining Loyalty, Achieving Profitability, and Adding Value as a Consultant - $27.95
- <u>CEO Leadership Strategies</u> - Key Methods and Traits for Business Success - $49.95
- <u>CEO Best Practices</u> - Skills, Values, and Strategies for Successful CEOs - $27.95
- <u>International Public Relations</u> - Successful Public Relations Techniques for Use in Major Markets Around the Globe - $219.95
- <u>Inside the Minds: Public Relations Best Practices</u> - Industry Insiders Offer Proven Tips for the Most Effective Communications Strategies - $27.95
- <u>CMO Leadership Strategies</u> - Top Executives from ABC, Time Warner, and More on Creating and Delivering Successful Marketing Campaigns That Impact the Bottom Line - $49.95
- <u>Sales Leadership Strategies</u> - Top Vice Presidents on Increasing Sales and Inspiring Your Team - $27.95
- <u>Getting Your Message Across</u> - IR and PR Executives Offer Leadership Strategies and Keys to Success - $27.95

Other Best Sellers

- Ninety-Six and Too Busy to Die - Life Beyond the Age of Dying - $24.95
- Technology Blueprints - Strategies for Optimizing and Aligning Technology Strategy and Business - $69.95
- The CEO's Guide to Information Availability - Why Keeping People and Information Connected is Every Leader's New Priority - $27.95
- Being There Without Going There - Managing Teams Across Time Zones, Locations, and Corporate Boundaries - $24.95
- Profitable Customer Relationships - CEOs from Leading Software Companies on Using Technology to Maximize Acquisition, Retention, and Loyalty - $27.95
- The Entrepreneurial Problem Solver - Leading CEOs on How to Think Like an Entrepreneur and Solve Any Problem for Your Team/Company - $27.95
- The Philanthropic Executive - Establishing a Charitable Plan for Individuals and Businesses - $27.95
- The Golf Course Locator for Business Professionals - Organized by Closest to Largest 500 Companies, Cities, and Airports - $12.95
- Living Longer Working Stronger - Seven Steps to Capitalizing on Better Health - $14.95
- Business Travel Bible - Must-Have Phone Numbers, Business Resources, Maps, and Emergency Info - $19.95
- ExecRecs - Executive Recommendations for the Best Business Products and Services Professionals Use to Excel - $14.95